Bonfire of Illusions

The Twin Crises of the Liberal World

— Alex Callinicos —

polity

First published in 2010 by Polity Press
Reprinted 2010 (twice), 2011

Polity Press
65 Bridge Street
Cambridge CB2 1UR, UK

Polity Press
350 Main Street
Malden, MA 02148, USA

ISBN-13: 978-0-7456-4875-0 (hardback)
ISBN-13: 978-0-7456-4876-7(paperback)

A catalogue record for this book is available from the British Library.

Typeset in 11 on 13 pt Sabon
by Toppan Best-set Premedia Limited
Printed and bound in Great Britain by the MPG Books Group

For further information on Polity, visit our website: www.politybooks.com

In Memoriam

Peter Gowan
(1946–2009)

Chris Harman
(1942–2009)

'One must always try to be as radical as reality itself.'

V. I. Lenin

Contents

Conclusion: Regime Change or System Change?   127

Preface and Acknowledgements

I must confess to having had some second thoughts about the title of this book. The illusions that I had in mind were those forming the dominant ideology in the era since the end of the Cold War, and crucially the belief – most famously articulated by Francis Fukuyama when he announced the End of History in 1989 – that liberal capitalism offered the only basis on which humankind could hope to enjoy peace, prosperity and freedom. The starting point of this book is that this belief was exposed as illusory in the late summer and autumn of 2008, with the geopolitical setback suffered by the United States in the war between Russia and Georgia and the economic earthquake unleashed by the collapse of Lehman Brothers on 15 September 2008.

I still think that this is right, and indeed in this book I develop an extensive analysis in support based in particular on the long-term crisis of overaccumulation and profitability from which the advanced capitalist economies have been suffering for several decades. But I forgot the point that Marx made when he pointed out the limits of any purely intellectual critique of the religious beliefs people have: 'To call them to give up their illusions about their condition is to *call on them to give up a condition that requires illusions.'*

Thus, despite the enormous material and symbolic blows that it has suffered, liberal capitalism attempts to steam ahead as if nothing happened. According to a study by the Bank of England published in November 2009, the state bailouts of the financial system have cost $14 trillion in the US, Britain and the euro-zone, nearly a quarter of global output. Yet governments still seek to propitiate the financial markets whose continued survival depends on their own efforts. Public services are butchered in the drive to return to neoliberal 'normality'. Most absurdly, market solutions are proposed to the enormous problem of global warming.

And so the illusions have survived the bonfire. This is an exercise in collective deception and self-deception, but it indicates that we are dealing with illusions sustained by material interests. They are, in other words, a symptom of 'a condition that requires illusions'. This makes ending that condition all the more urgent. The shambles of the Copenhagen climate summit in December 2009, which was torpedoed by cynical manoeuvres between the major powers, underlines how important it is to rid the world of an economic system driven by blind competition among firms and states.

In writing this book I have, of course, depended on others. At Polity I benefited from the support and assistance of Clare Ansell, Susan Beer, David Held and Sarah Lambert. Sam Ashman, Joseph Choonara and Chris Harman all read the book in draft and made very valuable comments. Lorenzo Fusaro helped me see the importance of David Harvey's *The Limits to Capital* in integrating different partial perspectives on capitalism. I would like to thank them all for the help they have given me though naturally they are not responsible for the use I have made of it.

The year 2009 took a terrible cull of Marxist intellectuals of the 1960s generation. We saw the passing, for example, of Giovanni Arrighi and Jerry Cohen. *Bonfire of Illusions* is dedicated to two others. In the past decade, Peter Gowan developed a critical political economy of the contemporary world that is both original and stimulating. Before that Peter had, among many other things, headed a sustained effort to promote the development of anti-Stalinist socialism in what was still the Soviet Union and Eastern Europe. I learned a great deal from reading and talking to Peter. He was a splendid human being and his death in June 2009 was a great loss.

But then, suddenly and unexpectedly, Chris Harman died in November 2009. This is a source of grief that I still find it hard to express. Chris had been both a friend and a pervasive intellectual influence for more than thirty-five years. While he developed Marxist thought in many different areas, his work in political economy was particularly important and helped very much to shape my own views on the subject. It is especially sad that Chris should have died at a time when his writing on Marxist political economy was so productive, as is evident in what proved to be his last book, *Zombie Capitalism*. I read and commented on it in draft, as he did for both this book and its predecessor, *Imperialism and Global Political Economy*. It seems quite impossible that our long dialogue is over and I must continue without him.

Introduction: How the World Changed in 2008

The proclamation of some event or date as marking a historic turning point – a great end or beginning – has a distinguished ancestry. It starts, perhaps, with Goethe, after the French revolutionary forces had overwhelmed the armies of the old regime at Valmy in September 1792, announcing: 'From this place and from this place forth commences a new era in the world's history.' But the practice has degenerated into the dullest of journalistic cliché, as the latest turn in fashion or in the political cycle is energetically spun as marking a profound discontinuity in historical time. No doubt at play here is one manifestation of the ideology of endless novelty that is an important aspect of how contemporary capitalism presents itself to the world.

All the same, just because this debasement has taken place doesn't mean that events of a genuinely epochal character never take place.[1] In my view, the late summer and early autumn of 2008 marked just such an event. Its nature is indicated by two episodes in particular; first, the brief war between Russia and Georgia in early August, and then, the collapse on Lehman Brothers on 15 September, which promptly precipitated the biggest global financial

crash since the Great Depression of the 1930s. What
event do these episodes – themselves of unequal significance, the second of greater import than the first – help
to mark?

A first approximation would be to say that they indicate
the end of the post-Cold War era. This goes against the
common view that it was the terrorist attacks on New
York and Washington on 11 September 2001 that brought
this period to a close. But, when one thinks about it, this
standard account isn't really right. For the reunification of
Europe on Western terms and the collapse of the Soviet
Union opened a period of unprecedented supremacy by the
United States in the interstate system. The ideological
accompaniment of this American primacy – most influen-
tially articulated by Francis Fukuyama in his theory of
'The End of History' – could be summed up in two propositions: that liberal capitalism was the only rationally
acceptable socio-economic framework for a modern society
and that a widening circle of liberal democracies could
offer the world benign global governance. There were
variations in how these propositions were articulated and
pursued, but they constituted a common sense shared by
the leaderships of the main Western states.[2]

A particular kind of challenge to this ideological and
political constellation was dramatized by the 9/11 attacks,
but they didn't disperse it. On the contrary, in its response
to the attacks, the administration of George W. Bush
sought strenuously to reaffirm and reinforce US hegemony
– and, indeed, the apparently speedy victories it initially
won in both Afghanistan and Iraq led many to believe that
it was succeeding in this enterprise. Moreover, the US
under the younger Bush reasserted the neoliberal triumphalism that had been the consensual view of the Western
ruling classes since 1989. The administration's notorious
National Security Strategy, published in the interlude
between the evictions of the Taliban and that of Saddam
Hussein, began by affirming the outcome of the Cold War
had left 'a single sustainable model for national success:

freedom, democracy, and free enterprise'.[3] Other Western states might jib at the Bush administration's unilateralism, and, in some cases, defend somewhat different models of liberal capitalism from the free-market version the US was widely seen as embodying. But the commitment that the European Union showed to the Doha round of trade liberalization negotiations, launched by the World Trade Organization in November 2001 in part as a riposte to 9/11, indicated that the disagreements at the level of principle were comparatively slight (though the conflicts of interest dividing it from the US were, as the endlessly stalemated talks showed, quite another matter).

So why did 2008 mark a break from this pattern? Let's consider the war between Russia and Georgia first. On the face of it, this was a territorial conflict of a rather traditional kind between a Russian state that regards itself as the residuary legatee of the Tsarist and Soviet empires and a Georgian government eager to reclaim the Moscow-backed separatist enclaves of South Ossetia and Abkhazia. But the Georgian President, Mikheil Saakashvili, had, ever since the 'Rose Revolution' of November 2003 that brought him to power, presented his regime as what the *Financial Times* calls 'an outpost of Euro-Atlanticism' in the Caucasus, campaigning for admission to the North Atlantic Treaty Organization (NATO) and training and equipping his army with the assistance of the US and Israel. It seems probable that, in attacking the South Ossetian capital of Tskhinvali on 7 August 2008, Saakashvili blundered into 'a well laid Russian trap', as the *Financial Times* put it. In other words, the Russian President, Dimitri Medvedev, and his over-mighty Prime Minister, Vladimir Putin, used the war to inflict a crushing military defeat on Georgia and thereby to demonstrate their determination to resist Washington's efforts to expand NATO eastwards till it encircled Russia.[4]

So the Russia–Georgia war was about more than an obscure territorial dispute in Moscow's near-abroad. The intelligence consultant George Friedman interprets a speech

made by Medvedev in the immediate aftermath of the war
as expressing the broadest geopolitical objectives:

> Medvedev is saying that Russia is engaged in a general
> redefinition of the regional and global system. Locally, it
> would not be correct to say that Russia is trying to resur-
> rect the Soviet Union or the Russian empire. It would be
> correct to say that Russia is creating a new structure of
> relations in the geography of its predecessors, with a new
> institutional structure with Moscow at its centre.
>
> Globally, the Russians want to use this new regional power
> – and substantial Russian nuclear assets – to be part of a
> global system in which the United States loses its primacy.[5]

Friedman argues that this Russian strategy depended on
exploiting the fact that the US is so heavily committed in
Iraq and Afghanistan that it lacks the military capabilities
to deal with crises in other regions:

> the United States had created a massive window of oppor-
> tunity for the Russians: For the foreseeable future, the
> United States had no significant forces to spare to deploy
> elsewhere in the world, nor the ability to sustain them in
> extended combat. Moreover, the United States was relying
> on Russian cooperation both against Iran and potentially
> in Afghanistan, where Moscow's influence with some fac-
> tions remains substantial.
>
> The United States needed the Russians and couldn't block
> the Russians.[6]

In other words, the war between Russia and Georgia made
visible what is now widely believed to be the major long-
term consequence of the Iraq war – namely that, far from
affirming and entrenching US primacy, the seizure of Iraq
at once exposed and magnified American weakness. The
late Giovanni Arrighi argued particularly forcefully that the
administration of the younger Bush marked 'the terminal
crisis of US hegemony'.[7] According to Oksana Antonenko,
senior fellow for Russia and Eurasia at the International

Institute of Strategic Studies in London, a similar view informed the attitude of the Medvedev–Putin partnership towards the US under the presidency of Barack Obama: 'there is an overwhelming view in Moscow now that the Americans are in decline and will be forced to negotiate with Russia from a position of weakness'.[8]

Moscow's new assertiveness, bolstered as it was by the vast foreign currency reserves it had accumulated thanks to the buoyancy of world prices for the oil and natural gas that were Russia's most important exports, encouraged speculation about the rise of 'authoritarian capitalisms' challenging both American hegemony and the neoliberal economic model it championed. After all, the prodigious Chinese boom so central to the world economy during the 2000s showed no sign of undermining the dominance of the Communist Party or weakening the reigning alliances between state managers, local entrepreneurs and transnational corporations.

But the apparent weakening or even demise of US hegemony is as intimately connected with the second episode as it is with the first. In September 2008, after the global financial crash precipitated by the collapse of Lehman's, leading European politicians were quick to argue that both neoliberalism and American primacy had been drastically weakened. The French President, Nicolas Sarkozy, declared: 'Laissez faire is finished. The all-powerful market which is always right is finished.' Peer Steinbrück, the German Finance Minister, was even blunter, telling the Bundestag: 'The US will lose its status as the superpower of the world financial system.'[9] But the belief – more accurately in this case, the fear – that the world economic crisis would weaken the US was shared on the other side of the Atlantic. Consider, for example, the reaction of Roger Altman, Deputy Treasury Secretary under Bill Clinton (though he seeks to associate the EU in the general wreck):

The financial and economic crash of 2008, the worst in over 75 years, is a major geopolitical setback for the United

States and Europe. Over the medium term, Washington
and European governments will have neither the resources
nor the economic credibility to play the role in global
affairs they otherwise would have played. These weaknesses will eventually be repaired, but in the interim, they
will accelerate trends that are shifting the world's centre
of gravity away from the United States.[10]

But, of course, the crash is significant for far more than its
geopolitical consequences. Indeed, while the Russian–
Georgian war was simply one step in a much longer term
geopolitical process of declining US power, the Lehman's
collapse and its aftermath marked a much more dramatic
turning point. What began as the bursting of a speculative
bubble in the US housing market in 2006–7 – the so-called
subprime crisis – and the credit crunch that followed it
have developed into a full-scale global economic and financial crisis marked by the first fall in global output since the
Second World War. Even if it may not prove as deep or
protracted as the Great Depression of the 1930s, the
present crisis invites comparison with the latter. The scale
of the catastrophe is all the more striking because it so
closely follows an era of capitalist triumphalism fuelled by
the credit boom of the mid-2000s. In his final budget in
March 2007, Gordon Brown, then British Chancellor of
the Exchequer and soon to become Prime Minister, boasted
of the strength of the economy and of public finances, and
declaimed: 'And we will never return to the old boom and
bust.'[11] In October of the same year, several months after
the outbreak of the subprime crisis, the International Monetary Fund compared the boom favourably with the Golden
Age of postwar capitalism during the Long Boom of the
1950s and 1960s:

> In recent years, output growth has been much more rapid
> than observed at any time since the oil shocks of the 1970s.
> Compared with the 1960s, however, neither the strength
> nor the length of the current expansion appears excep-
> tional. That said, rapid growth has been shared across

countries more broadly than in the past, and output volatility in most countries and regions has been significantly lower than during the 1960s.[12]

Within eighteen months the IMF had changed its tune, agonizing over the 'worrisome parallels' between the global economic and financial crisis and the Great Depression.[13] As the responses of Sarkozy and Steinbrück demonstrate, responsibility for the crisis is widely attributed to the deregulated, free-market version of liberal capitalism promoted by the US and Britain since the 1980s. Nevertheless, the very scale of the crisis invites, as it did in the case of its predecessor in the 1930s, reflection on the extent to which its causes are systemic, lying in the very nature of the capitalist mode of production.

Moreover, like the Great Depression, the current world economic crisis has precipitated dramatic policy reversals. In August 1929, the British Labour government collapsed in the face of a spreading international financial crisis and demands from the banks for drastic cuts in public spending. Its successor, a Tory-dominated National Government headed by the ex-Labour Prime Minister, Ramsay Mac-Donald, promptly took Britain off the gold standard. Sidney Webb, as Lord Passfield a member of the outgoing Labour cabinet, complained: 'Nobody told us we could do this.' This remark demonstrated the extent to which even one of the founders of the Fabian Society was a prisoner of the free-market orthodoxy of the day. But it also highlighted the dramatic shifts in policy and ideology underway. A. J. P. Taylor comments: 'A few days before, a managed currency had seemed as wicked as family planning. Now, like contraception, it became a commonplace.'[14] The Great Depression era was marked by states intervening far more intrusively into national economies and in some cases (notably Germany under Hitler and the Soviet Union under Stalin) assuming their overall direction.[15]

While so far the reaction to the global economic and financial crisis has not gone anywhere as far as the state capitalism of the 1930s, the direction is the same. The ideological reversal is brought out by a rather hubristic piece by the energetic Tory historian Niall Ferguson that appeared in the *Financial Times* in December 2007. As part of a clumsy attempt to use Darwin's theory of evolution by natural selection to analyse the working of the financial markets, Ferguson declared that 'the only species [of bank] that is now close to extinction in developed countries is the state-owned bank, as privatization has swept the world'.[16] This was an unwise thing to have written even at the time, since the New Labour government in Britain was already drafting legislation to nationalize Northern Rock, the bank that had been driven to collapse when the credit markets froze up the previous autumn. But Ferguson was soon to be spectacularly discomfited: the very governments at the heart of the deregulated global financial markets organized mammoth rescues of institutions bankrupted as the deflation of the credit bubble of the mid-2000s claimed more and more victims. These amounted to the greatest nationalizations in world history. In autumn 2008 the lame-duck Bush administration took over the mortgage companies Fannie Mae and Freddie Mac and the insurance giant AIG while the British government became a majority shareholder in the Royal Bank of Scotland (by assets, the largest company in the world) and Lloyds Banking Group. Now it was renationalization – and not of some bankrupt industrial firm but of the commanding heights of the financial system – that was sweeping the world.

The bank rescues were part of a much larger policy reversal, as the leading states poured unfathomable amounts of money into their banking systems and also increased spending and borrowing in order to counteract the dramatic falls in demand driving the world economy into a depression. The fact that the shift was most pronounced in the US and Britain, the very states where the push towards deregulation and privatization had been taken furthest (and pressed most aggressively on other countries), provoked disarray and some anger elsewhere. Neoliberalism proved to be for dummies – something that the states at the centre of the system imposed on others but didn't practise themselves when they got into economic difficulties. The Czech Prime Minister, Mirek Topolánek, whose government was then occupying the EU presidency, told the European Parliament in March 2009 that Obama's policy of seeking a global fiscal stimulus (tax cuts and public spending increases) and the US drift towards protectionism represented 'the road to hell'.[17] This rather undiplomatic remark by the head of a lame-duck Eurosceptic government chimed in with a broader hostility on the part of the leading states in the euro-zone – notably Germany and France – to the apparent conversion of the capitals of neoliberalism to Keynesianism. Steinbrück, for example, criticized the British Prime Minister, Gordon Brown, for cutting Value-Added Tax in an effort to stimulate demand: 'All this will do is raise Britain's debt to a level that will take a whole generation to work off. The same people who would never touch deficit spending are now tossing around billions. The switch from decades of supply-side politics all the way to a crass Keynesianism is breathtaking.'[18]

But the political disarray was closely associated with a major ideological crisis. Once again, this paralleled the 1930s, where what Maynard Keynes called the 'Treasury View' based on free-market orthodoxy came under sustained intellectual attack. The result was to legitimize alternative economic models – not merely the vision of a state-managed capitalism that Keynes himself outlined in *The General Theory of Employment, Interest and Money* (1936), but also different kinds of planned economy.[19] G. D. H. Cole wrote in 1937 in a mass-produced Penguin paperback: 'the alternatives are no longer State regulation and free competition, but planning under restrictive capitalist control and planning under public auspices, with a view to the maximum satisfaction of the consumers' needs'. After surveying the different attempts at planning in response to the Great Depression – in the Soviet Union, fascist Italy, Nazi Germany, the US under the New Deal, and Tory Britain, Cole concluded: 'In only one of the five countries that I have attempted to study is there any attempt to plan for the full use of the available resources of production in meeting the demands of human welfare. That country is, of course, the one Socialist country – the USSR.'[20]

It was the progressive stagnation of the Stalinist command economy, along with the failure of Keynesian demand management to prevent the return of major economic crises in the 1970s and 1980s, that helped to create the conditions in which *laissez faire* economics could regain intellectual hegemony under the leadership of Milton Friedman and Friedrich von Hayek and legitimize the policies of the administrations of Ronald Reagan and Margaret Thatcher, generalized in the form of neoliberalism.[21] But the global economic crisis and the policy response it has evoked offer, to say the least, powerful evidence that the neoliberal economic policy regime has failed. Consequently the theories that legitimized this regime cannot escape critical interrogation about their contribution to the disaster.

Economics, which as an academic discipline has in recent decades clad itself in the armour of highly mathematized versions of neoclassical orthodoxy and refused to entertain heterodox approaches, has come under increasing attack. When the Queen visited the London School of Economics in December 2008 she asked: 'why did no one see it coming?' Alas, none of the culprits were hauled off to the Tower.[22] The challenge has, on the whole, come from outsiders like Her Majesty, or Nassim Nicholas Taleb, the conservative author of popular critiques of the self-delusions of financial-market actors. Taleb mounted a ferocious attack on financial economics and, in particular, modern portfolio theory:

> MPT is the foundation of works in economics and finance that several times received the Sveriges Riksbank Prize in Economic Sciences in Memory of Alfred Nobel. The prize

was created (and funded) by the Swedish central bank and has been progressively confused with the regular Nobel set up by Alfred Nobel; it is now mislabelled the 'Nobel Prize for Economics'.

MPT produces measures such as 'sigmas, 'betas, 'Sharpe ratios', 'correlation', 'value at risk', 'optimal portfolios' and 'capital asset pricing model' that are incompatible with the possibility of those consequential rare events I call 'black swans' (owing to their rarity, as most swans are white). So my problem is that the prize is not just an insult to science; it has been putting the financial system at risk of blow-ups . . . We learn from crisis to crisis that MPT has the empirical and scientific validity of astrology (without the aesthetics), yet the lessons are ignored in what is taught to 150,000 business school students worldwide.[23]

If anyone was awarded the booby prize for the financial crash it was Alan Greenspan. Greenspan, in his youth a member of the right-wing libertarian *groupuscule* led by Ayn Rand, graduated to becoming an economic adviser to Republican administrations and, finally, Chairman of the Federal Reserve Board, the American central bank, between 1987 and 2006. He was given much credit for the US economic expansion of the late 1990s, becoming the subject of a reverential portrait, *Maestro*, by Bob Woodward, the court historian of the American establishment. But, even before his retirement, Greenspan was coming under increasing fire for allowing speculative bubbles to develop in the stock and housing markets. These criticisms reached crescendo level once the financial markets froze in August 2007.

After the Lehman collapse and the ensuing crash, Greenspan appeared in October 2008 before a Congressional committee eager to track down the culprits responsible for the catastrophe. In a session that bore some resemblance to the auto-critiques by 'bourgeois' professors during the Chinese Cultural Revolution, Greenspan confessed his 'shocked disbelief' at the failure of financial markets to conform to his theories:

I made a mistake in presuming that the self-interest of
organizations, specifically banks and others, were such that
they were best capable of protecting their own sharehold-
ers and their equity in the firms . . . So the problem here is
something which looked to be a very solid edifice, and,
indeed, a critical pillar to market competition and free
markets, did break down. And I think that, as I said,
shocked me. I still do not fully understand why it happened
and, obviously, to the extent that I figure out where it
happened and why, I will change my views . . . yes, I found
a flaw, I don't know how significant or permanent it is,
but I have been very distressed by that fact.[24]

This is no minor 'flaw' that Greenspan acknowledges.
Neoclassical economics transformed into a dogma Adam
Smith's famous observation that the market actor who
'intends only his own gain' is often 'led by an invisible
hand to promote an end which was no part of his inten-
tion . . . By pursuing his own interest he frequently promotes that of the society more effectually than when he
really intends to promote it.'[25] The dogmatic version asserts
that leaving economic actors to follow their interests will
produce socially optimal outcomes: it was precisely this
claim that Keynes aimed to demolish in seeking to demonstrate that a market economy can reach equilibrium at
less than full employment. But now, the 'libertarian Republican' Alan Greenspan admits, the connection between
self-interest and the general welfare has broken down, at
least in the case of financial markets. The implications are
enormous, given the extent to which market solutions have
come to govern public policy in the neoliberal era, for
example, in the drive to privatize public services. Nor was
Greenspan alone. Josef Ackermann, chief executive of
Deutsche Bank, declared a few months earlier: 'I no longer
believe in the market's self-healing power.'[26]

Others were not so prepared to concede intellectual
defeat. Launching with much fanfare an ambitious series
on 'The Future of Capitalism' in the spring of 2009, the
Financial Times sought to prejudge the outcome of the

debate. The problem lay in 'an un-transparent financial sector', where derivatives such as credit default swaps and collateralized debt obligations circulated without receiving an accurate valuation in functioning markets, a practice 'akin to peddling tulips with equations':

> Those who sound the death knell of market capitalism are therefore mistaken. This was not a failure of markets; it was a failure to create proper markets. What is to blame is a certain mindset, embodied not least by Mr Greenspan. It ignored a capitalist economy's inherent instabilities – and therefore relieved policymakers who could manage those instabilities of their responsibility to do so. This is not the bankruptcy of a social system, but the intellectual and moral failure of those who were in charge of it: a failure for which there is no excuse.[27]

The conclusion – that the problem was not the system but its managers – was muddled by the reference to 'a capitalist economy's inherent instabilities', which seems hardly consistent with the idea that 'proper markets' are crisis-free. A more coherent response, though not one marked by the willingness to acknowledge error displayed by Greenspan, was offered by the *Financial Times*'s chief economic commentator, Martin Wolf. A few years before the outbreak of the global economic and financial crisis, Wolf had published an aggressive defence of neoliberal globalization called *Why Globalization Works*. In it he was particularly concerned to parry the attacks mounted by Joseph Stiglitz and more radical critics on the financial liberalization pressed on 'emerging market economies' in central and eastern Europe and the global South in the 1980s and 1990s and widely seen as the major cause of the East Asian crisis. Acknowledging that the neoliberal era has seen a sharp increase in the number of financial crises, Wolf nevertheless insisted: 'Massive financial crises are not inevitable.' Indeed, 'there is good reason to believe' that 'the propensity to crisis could be reduced'.[28] In a subsequent study devoted specifically to the problem of

financial crises that was written before the onset of the
world economic crisis but published just after the financial
crash of autumn 2008, Wolf still treated them as a phenomenon of the periphery of the global system.[29]

Confronted with a crisis at the very heart of that system,
he quickly shed his old intellectual garments. He now
declared that 'Keynes offers us the best way to think about
the financial crisis', and praised the post-Keynesian economist Hyman Minsky, whose analysis of the inherent instability of financial markets has suddenly become very
fashionable.[30] Accordingly Wolf attacked the free-marke-
teers who argued that a deep recession would restore the
world economy to health and pressed for the leading states
to 'do more than enough' to maintain effective demand
through much more ambitious fiscal stimulus packages
than they had already introduced.[31] His *Financial Times*
colleague Samuel Brittan, who had played a key role during
the 1970s in converting the British establishment to Friedman's monetarism, went even further, declaring 'Keynes,
thou should'st be living . . .' and replying to critics of fiscal
stimuli who asked where the money would come from:
'The short answer is: the Bank of England printing works
in Debden.'[32]

Intellectual somersaults of this kind were to a significant
extent a tribute to the severity of the economic crisis. Business as usual – the normal workings of market capitalism
– could be suspended for the duration of the economic
emergency. All the same, the effect of the policy and ideological reversals was to widen the boundaries of the possible. One of the main effects of neoliberalism has been to
renaturalize economic relations. Even if it was intended
to rescue capitalism from its worst crisis, the Keynesian
revolution legitimized the idea of political control of the
economy. The lesson of the Phillips curve, for example,
which posits a trade-off between inflation and unemployment, was that governments, depending on their political
coloration, could choose the mix of inflation and unemployment that best reflected their values and priorities.

This implied that economic relations were not governed by autonomous mechanisms resembling those driving physical processes.[33]

One of Friedman's key interventions was directed against the Phillips curve and was intended to demonstrate that a market economy would tend to gravitate towards a 'natural' rate of unemployment determined crucially by the cost, productivity and distribution of labour. Beyond the very short term, governments could not affect the rate of unemployment, but merely, if they increased spending and cut taxes in an effort to run the economy at a lower level of unemployment than the natural rate and thereby expanded the money supply, push up the rate of inflation. This argument served to legitimize the renunciation of Keynesian demand management and the pursuit of monetary and fiscal stability, eventually through the transfer of control over interest rates to independent central banks, that were key features of the neoliberal economic policy regime as it took shape in the 1980s and 1990s. The aim was to return the economy to the kind of autopilot that it was on during the era of the gold standard in the nineteenth and early twentieth centuries – what Hayek called 'get[ting] back some more or less automatic system for regulating the quantity of money'.[34] The major premiss of the Third Way – the attempt by Tony Blair, Bill Clinton and others to marry the centre left to neoliberalism – was an acceptance of this renaturalization of economic relations.[35]

The development of the financial crisis after August 2007 sent all this to the four winds. As central banks pushed interest rates close to zero in an effort to counter recessionary forces, monetary policy became inoperative. Now it was fiscal policy that became crucial, resting on the very power of the state to tax and spend that it had been one of the main aims of neoliberalism to limit and restrict. Even the central bank's use of 'quantitative easing' – the purchase of government and corporate bonds to pump more money into the financial system and keep interest rates low – depended on the state as the issuer of the fiat money used in these purchases. This was no mere technical question of policy instruments. The resort to fiscal stimuli demonstrated the ability of states to generate variant outcomes, reflected in the fact that some were more willing to borrow and spend than others. In the process, economic relations were being denaturalized once again. The autopilot had been switched off: politics was at the controls of the world economy.

This posed the question of what would happen once the crisis was over. Would the autopilot be put back in charge again? Or had it been exposed – like the chess-playing automaton of which Walter Benjamin tells at the start of his 'Theses on the Philosophy of History', which was really operated by 'a little hunchback who was an expert chess player' – not to be a physical mechanism after all, but to be directed by human agents with their own interests?[36] Certainly many of the champions of neoliberalism were afraid that there would be no return to business as usual. The *Economist*, for example, warned that the 'deglobalization' advocated by the anti-globalization intellectual and activist Walden Bello might be taking place: 'the process [of globalization] is going into reverse. Globalization means the global integration of the movement of goods, capital, and jobs. Each of these processes is now in trouble', as international trade and foreign direct investment shrank under the impact of the world crisis.[37]

Another, more positive way of putting it would be to say that the effect of both the crisis and the responses to it has been to show us that a far wider range of possibilities is open to us than the established economic and political consensus had allowed us previously to entertain. So Passfield's complaint – 'Nobody told us we could do this' – has powerful contemporary resonances. The fury of right-wing Republicans in Congress at the state rescues of the banking system – Senator Jim Bunning of Kentucky called the $700bn Troubled Assets Rescue Programme introduced by the Bush administration after the Lehman's collapse 'financial socialism, it is un-American' – is therefore entirely intelligible.[38] Options that they had thought had been long foreclosed have suddenly re-emerged into the full light of day.

In a fine piece written in response to Obama's election victory – which, he said, whatever reservations one might have about the actual policies Obama would pursue, 'widens our freedom and thereby the scope of our decisions' – Slavoj Žižek warned that which alternative eventually prevailed politically would depend on the power of different interpretations of the economic and financial crisis:

> It is unlikely that the financial meltdown of 2008 will function as a blessing in disguise, the awakening from a dream, the sobering reminder that we live in the reality of global capitalism. It all depends on how it will be symbolized, on what ideological interpretation or story will impose itself and determine the general perception of the crisis. When the normal run of things is traumatically interrupted, the field is open for a 'discursive' ideological competition. In Germany in the late 1920s, Hitler won the competition to determine which narrative would explain the reasons for the crisis of the Weimar Republic and the way out of it; in France in 1940 Maréchal Pétain's narrative won in the contest to find the reasons for the French defeat. Consequently, to put it in old-fashioned Marxist terms, the main task of the ruling ideology in the present crisis is to impose a narrative that will not put the blame for the meltdown on the global capitalist system as such, but on its deviations – lax regulation, the corruption of big financial institutions etc . . . The danger is thus that the predominant narrative of the meltdown won't be the one that awakes us from a dream, but the one that will enable us to continue to dream.[39]

But what then is the best 'narrative of the meltdown'? To put it a little differently, what is the best theoretical framework to make sense of the economic and political upheavals under way? In autobiographical mood, Martin Wolf has told us that, as a student at Oxford in the 1960s,

'I already knew that all the varieties of Marxism were both wicked and stupid.'[40] But those less inclined to prejudge the issue might think the present to be quite a good moment to take a look at the kind of take that Marxism offers on the contemporary world. After all, Marxist political economy has developed a considerable body of analysis that seeks to unravel the constitutive instabilities of capitalism as an economic system. Moreover, it has, ever since the early years of the twentieth century, been intimately interconnected with the attempt to develop a theory of imperialism that seeks to grasp the deep relationship between economic and geopolitical competition under capitalism.[41] This might seem to make Marxism particularly helpful in unravelling the perplexities of a world in dramatic flux both economically and geopolitically.

In any case, it is Marxist political economy that informs and organizes this book. What does this mean? In many ways Marx's most important insight lay in conceiving, as he put it, capital as a social relation. To put it more formally, the capitalist mode of production is constituted by two antagonistic social relationships (or structural contradictions), namely that between capital and wage-labour and that between capitals themselves. The first is one of exploitation: it is labour that, in the course of producing new commodities, creates new value and is therefore the source of the profits that provide capitals with both their fuel and their measure of success; this surplus-value is appropriated by capital thanks to its control of the process of production. This contradiction, because it constitutes capital as dependent on the appropriation of surplus-labour, is the more fundamental of the two, but it is incomplete without the second. Capital as such is only an abstraction; what actually exists are individual capitals competing with one another as each seeks to maximize its share of the surplus-value they jointly extract from workers. It is the pressure of competition that compels capitals to achieve a certain level of exploitation and also to accumulate, reinvesting surplus-value in expanding and improving their productive capabilities. But this process of competitive accumulation is responsible for the tendency towards regular and profound economic crises that Marx believes to be inherent in the capitalist mode of production and the clearest evidence of its historically limited and transitory character.[42]

The preceding paragraph is a very brief summary of a complicated and abstract theory. I hope in the chapters that follow to demonstrate the value of Marxist political economy as a means of illuminating the world today. The book's structure is simple enough. In Chapter 1, I consider the dynamics of the world economic and financial crisis. My particular concern will be to explore the extent to which the financial collapse can be traced to deeper structures and tendencies of contemporary capitalism. This will involve considering some of the theories that have been developed to analyse financial crises. Chapter 2, by contrast, is concerned with the domain of geopolitics, and in particular with the way in which the complicated interaction between the economic and financial crisis and the longer-term redistribution of global economic power that is under way is influencing the relative capabilities of the leading states. Finally, in the Conclusion, I discuss the possible political responses. Should we be seeking a return to neoliberal normality? Should we instead construct a policy regime that would return the world to a more regulated form of capitalism? Or should we aim to go beyond capitalism altogether?

− 1 −

Finance Humbled

I would rather see Finance less proud and Industry more content.'[1]

Winston Churchill, then British Chancellor of the Exchequer, wrote these words in February 1925, during the intense policy debates that led to the economically and politically disastrous decision to return the pound sterling to the gold standard at the exchange rate with the American dollar that had prevailed before the outbreak of the First World War. If the return to gold reflected 'Finance', in the shape of the City of London and Wall Street, at its proudest, the 1930s certainly saw it humbled. Nation-states responded to the Great Depression by managing their currencies, tightly restricting their financial markets, and more broadly regulating their economies in order, in particular, to promote the development of industry, often for strategic reasons. Franklin Roosevelt's New Deal administration directed heavy political fire at the Wall Street bankers. The great House of Morgan, which had played a crucial role in orchestrating Britain's return to gold, was the main target of Congressional hearings into Wall Street held in May 1933. These led to the passage of the Glass–Steagall Act 1933, which sought to restrict the speculative excesses of the financial markets, in particular by separating commercial and investment banking.[2]

Today finance is in the dock once again. Immense popular anger has been directed at the banks for their role in precipitating the global economic crisis. The revelation in March 2009 that Wall Street banks had paid out $18bn in year-end bonuses to their New York employees in 2008, after the federal government had pumped in $243bn to bail out the financial system, provoked a particularly fierce outburst of fury. Once again, Congressional hearings provided an arena where the culprits could be held to account. The pasting that Richard Fuld, Chief Executive Officer of Lehman Brothers, received at the hands of the House Oversight and Government Reform Committee (which a few weeks later provided the occasion for Alan Greenspan's self-criticism session) in October 2008 was particularly memorable. But perhaps the most satisfying scene of populist justice came – appropriately enough in the society of the spectacle – on *The Daily Show* in March 2009, when the comic Jon Stewart humiliated Jim Cramer, ex-hedge fund boss and presenter of CNBC's *Mad Money*, who cringed and squirmed as he desperately tried to ingratiate himself to his inquisitor and the studio audience. In Britain, the generous pension awarded to Sir Fred Goodwin, the disgraced ex-CEO of the bankrupt and nationalized Royal Bank of Scotland, became a comparable focus of parliamentary and media attack.

But it would be a serious mistake to reduce the fire directed at Wall Street and the City to such performances in a popular theatre of symbolic justice. The critique of finance was much more widely shared, in often surprising quarters. Consider, for example, this diagnosis by Simon Johnson, formerly chief economist of the International Monetary Fund:

In its depth and suddenness, the US economic and financial crisis is shockingly reminiscent of moments we have recently seen in emerging markets (and only in emerging markets): South Korea (1997), Malaysia (1998), Russia and Argentina (time and again). In each of those cases, global investors, afraid that the country or its financial sector wouldn't be able to pay off mountainous debt, suddenly stopped lending. And in each case, that fear became self-fulfilling, as banks that couldn't roll over their debt did, in fact, become unable to pay. This is precisely what drove Lehman Brothers into bankruptcy on September 15 [2008], causing all sources of funding to the US financial sector to dry up overnight. Just as in emerging-market crises, the weakness in the banking system has quickly rippled out into the rest of the economy, causing a severe economic contraction and hardship for millions of people.

But there's a deeper and more disturbing similarity: elite business interests – financiers, in the case of the US – played a central role in creating the crisis, making ever-larger gambles, with the implicit backing of the government, until the inevitable collapse. More alarming, they are now using their influence to prevent precisely the sorts of reforms that are needed, and fast, to pull the economy out of its nosedive. The government seems helpless, or unwilling, to act against them.[3]

Johnson offers an insider's view of the working of what he calls the world's 'most advanced oligarchy', in which

> the American financial industry gained political power by amassing a kind of cultural capital . . . Wall Street is a very seductive place, imbued with an air of power. Its executives truly believe that they control the levers that make the world go round. A civil servant from Washington invited into their conference rooms, even if just for a meeting, could be forgiven for falling under their sway. Throughout my time at the IMF, I was struck by the easy access of leading financiers to the highest US government officials, and the interweaving of the two career tracks. I vividly remember a meeting in early 2008 – attended by top policy makers from a handful of rich countries – at which the chair casually proclaimed, to the room's general approval, that the best preparation for becoming a central-bank governor was to work first as an investment banker.[4]

What is interesting is how closely Johnson's analysis parallels that offered by radical critics, for example, the late Peter Gowan, who lays responsibility for the crisis at the door of what he calls the 'New Wall Street System' that emerged in the past twenty-five years and is dominated by the investment banks and by shadow banks such as hedge funds and private equity firms.[5] But properly to assess such claims presupposes an understanding of the role played by finance in contemporary capitalism and of the dynamics of financial crises. It is towards establishing such an understanding that this chapter is largely devoted.

What is financialization?

Notoriously the global economic and financial crisis started in the subprime market in the US, where mortgages were provided to low-income households, often with what amounted to a fraudulent failure to check the borrowers' ability to make the repayments, especially when these were 'reset' – that is, when the initially low interest rate offered to attract borrowers was raised. These origins have themselves become the object of a highly politicized debate in the US, with the Republicans accusing the Democrats and the quasi-public mortgage companies Fannie Mae and Freddie Mac of having debauched the country's finances by encouraging cheap housing loans to the poor, and especially African-Americans. The real picture, as Gary Dymski has shown, was one of the rapid growth of 'predatory lending' during the 1990s and 2000s – financial firms selling 'mortgages with excessively high fees, penalties, and interest rates' to poor black households.[6] Greenspan in his memoirs embraces dodgy mortgages for the poor for the political project of the free-market right:

> I was aware that the loosening of mortgage credit terms for subprime borrowers increased financial risk, and that subsidized home ownership initiatives distort market out-

comes. But I believed then, as now, that the benefits of broadened home ownership are worth the risk. Protection of property rights, so critical to a market economy, requires a critical mass of owners to sustain political support.[7]

The expansion of the subprime market symbolized a much broader process of financialization in advanced capitalist societies, as even the poorest became identified as worthwhile – that is, profitable – people to lend money to. The idea that contemporary capitalism is characterized particularly by financialization has become a widely accepted view on the radical left in recent decades, and is now migrating to the mainstream, as the example of Johnson illustrates. But what is financialization? It is important to distinguish a number of different meanings concealed by the term. Three in particular stand out.[8]

The first is the view that finance – more specifically in the shape of the banks – is economically dominant. Thus two Marxist economists, Gérard Duménil and Dominique Lévy, interpret neoliberalism as 'the restoration of the hegemony of finance'.[9] This is sometimes articulated (though not in the case of Duménil and Lévy) by appeal to the authority of Rudolf Hilferding's theory of finance capital, first formulated before the First World War. According to Hilferding, the progressive concentration and centralization of capital that is one of the main tendencies of capitalist development isolated by Marx leads to a fusion of banking and industrial capital under the dominance of the former.[10] The theory is suggestive, but historically limited, since it generalizes from the specific pattern of capitalist development in Germany and the US in the late nineteenth and early twentieth centuries. Here small numbers of investment banks came to play a dominant economic role, thanks to the dependence of industrial firms on them to mobilize the capital required to invest on a scale necessary to overcome Britain's inherited competitive advantage. A version of this kind of 'coordinated capitalism', based on tight networks integrating investment banks and industrial firms, continues to prevail in Germany and Japan, but it never took hold in Britain and declined in the US after 1945.

Ron Chernow has written a fascinating history of J. P. Morgan and Co, which at the apogee of its power at the end of the nineteenth century used its access to capital (often British) to organize the construction of huge industrial cartels such as US Steel. He writes:

> The banker had grown powerful when capital markets were limited, with few financial intermediaries to tap them. In the post-World War II, however, capital markets would burgeon and become globally integrated. At the same time, the financial field would grow crowded with commercial banks, investment banks, insurance companies, brokerage houses, foreign banks, government lending programmes, multilateral organizations, and myriad other lenders. Gradually Wall Street bankers would lose their unique place in finance. Never again would a private bank such as J. P. Morgan be the most powerful agency on earth. Far from standing guard over scarce resources, bankers would evolve into glad-handing salesmen, almost pushing the bountiful stuff on customers.[11]

One symptom of the changed relationship between banks and industrial firms is provided by the tendency for the latter to finance their investments from retained profits.[12] Figure 1.1 highlights national variations: reliance on bank credit is high in Japan and Germany, where tight networks continue to bind investment banks and industrial firms together. But the marginal importance of bank credit to corporate finance in the US, the heartland of neoliberalism, is striking. François Chesnais, in a nuanced and detailed account of the development of what he calls a globalized regime of accumulation under financial domination, argues that it involves the emergence of industrial firms as autonomous financial actors:

> The formation of a market in loans packaged as securities ('securitization') has offered the big firms the possibility of

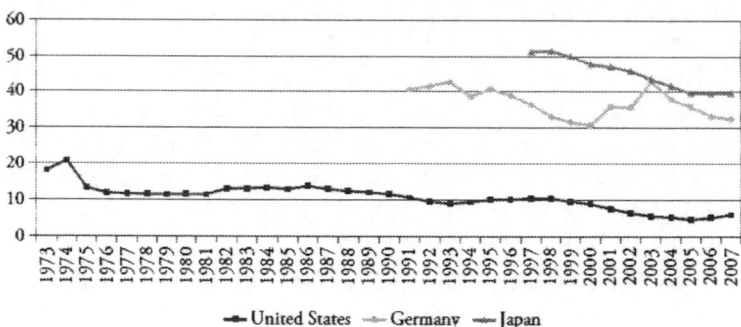

−■− United States ∼∞∼ Germany −∞− Japan

Figure 1.1 Bank Loans as Percentage of Corporate Liabilities, 1973–2007
Source: C. Lapavitsas, 'Financialized Capitalism: Crisis and Expropriation', *Historical Materialism*, 17.2 (2009), Figure 1, p. 115

freeing themselves, at least in part, from their dependence on bank credit. Since the middle of the 1980s, they have regularly issued as well as certificates of deposit their own medium-term corporate bonds. It is a matter of autonomy and of the freedom to manage as well as of the cost of the funds raised.[13]

The other side to the autonomy of industrial capital is that of finance itself. This suggests a second meaning of financialization, ably stated by Costa Lapavitsas:

> Financialization, in short, does not amount to dominance of banks over industrial and commercial capital. It stands rather for increasing autonomy of the financial sector. Industrial and commercial capitals are able to borrow in open financial markets, while being more heavily implicated in financial transactions. Meanwhile, financial institutions have sought new sources of profitability in personal income and financial market mediation.[14]

The ability of industrial and commercial firms to fund their own investments without resort to the banks helps to explain the proselytizing activities that led financial institutions to shove housing loans at America's poor. No longer having the fees and interest on industrial loans as a reliable source of profits, the banks turned elsewhere. But it is important to include here as well the proliferation of financial-market actors. Crucially, during the credit boom of the mid-2000s that forms the background to the present crisis, to the institutions listed by Chernow must be added the shadow banking sector – hedge funds, private equity firms, structured investment vehicles (SIVs). What these institutions have in common with more traditional investment banks is that, in conditions where credit was very cheap, they borrowed in order to trade in assets with the aim of making large short-term profits. Private equity firms, for example, specialize in acquiring publicly listed companies, taking them off the stock market and reorganizing them in order to increase their profitability (in the process closing down those parts where the returns were too low), and then selling them off at a substantial profit. As Adair Turner (who took over as head of the British Financial Services Authority during the credit crunch) notes, US mutual funds also started to operate more like banks, holding 'long-term credit assets against liabilities to investors which promise immediate redemption . . . As a result, their behaviour in a liquidity crisis – selling assets rapidly to meet redemptions – has become bank like in nature, contributing to systemic liquidity strains.'[15]

The economic function of the shadow banks is little different from that of investment banks proper, which in the neoliberal era have been making an increasingly high proportion of their profits from 'proprietary trading' – that is, through engaging in financial speculation on their own account rather than on behalf of their clients. But, while commercial and investment banks are subject to state regulation, hedge funds and the like have largely gone unregulated. This difference has been crucial in binding together the official and shadow banks in what proved to be a disastrous relationship. Under the Basel framework established through the Bank for International Settlements, banks are required to hold a certain amount of capital as security against their borrowers defaulting. Regulatory changes during the neoliberal era reduced the required leverage ratio between banks' assets (the loans they make) and equity (capital). In the drive to maximize profits, Gowan observes, '[t]he investment banks used their leverage ratio as the target to be achieved at all times rather than as an outer limit of risk to be reduced where possible by holding surplus capital'.[16]

This strategy gave banks a powerful incentive to pass as many loans as possible on to other institutions, notably structured investment vehicles, as a means off keeping them off the banks' balance sheets and transferring the risk of default elsewhere. This system of what Paul Tucker of the Bank of England calls 'vehicular finance' expanded enormously during the credit boom. The asset-backed commercial paper market that provided most of the funding for SIVs, after fluctuating around $600–700bn in the early 2000s, took off in 2004 and peaked at almost $1,200bn in the summer of 2007.[17] Mortgages of different kinds were packaged together into collateralized debt obligations (CDOs) and sold on as quickly as possible by the banks that had made the original housing loans. According to Bill Gross of the Pimco asset management group, the shadow banking system 'has lain hidden for years, untouched by regulation, yet free to magically and mystically create and then package subprime loans into a host of three-letter conduits that only Wall Street wizards could explain'.[18]

These new credit derivatives were praised for the way in which they spread risk. Greenspan declared in September 2002: 'If risk is properly dispersed, shocks to the overall economic system will be better absorbed and less likely to create cascading failures that could threaten financial stability.'[19] The IMF echoed him in April 2006:

> There is growing recognition that the dispersion of credit risk by banks to a broader and more diverse group of investors, rather than warehousing such risk on their

balance sheets, has helped to make the banking and overall financial system more resilient . . . Consequently, the commercial banks, a core segment of the financial system, may be less vulnerable today to credit or economic shocks.'[20]

But this particular brilliance of the system – the wide dispersion of risk – played a critical role in unleashing the present financial catastrophe. It meant that, when the US subprime market collapsed in 2006–7, banks especially in Europe – for example, Deutsche Bank, UBS and Royal Bank of Scotland – that had not been directly involved in this market were sucked in through their involvement with CDOs. The problem was intensified because the shadow banks underpinned their massive borrowing with lines of credit to mainstream banks, who therefore found themselves dragged into rescuing collapsing SIVs and taking loans that they thought they had sold on back onto their balance sheets. One of the biggest banks, Citigroup, went even further, promising to buy back super-senior CDOs from SIVs reluctant to take them on because they were (or so it was thought) low-risk and hence low-profit, a policy that caused devastating losses when the CDO market collapsed in the summer and autumn of 2007.[21]

The above tells us something about how a self-driven and dysfunctional financial sector blew itself – and the world economy – up. It is, however, critical to understand the economic and political context that allowed this to happen. Before doing so, however, we must distinguish a third meaning of financialization, namely the integration of a wider range of agents in financial markets – alongside the banks proper and the denizens of the shadow banking underworld, industrial and commercial capitalists, and also working-class households. In other words, it is important to distinguish between financial markets as an economic structure and financial institutions as a specific set of economic actors. As we have seen, one important feature of contemporary capitalism is that industrial and commercial firms raise money directly in financial markets by, for example, issuing bonds and certificates of deposit. Another feature is the provision of credit to individual consumers through mortgages, credit cards and the like. In this respect, finance has spread to entangle all economic actors in its nets.[22]

Marxist political economy can provide a theoretical framework for understanding this development. In *Capital* Volume III Marx distinguishes between three kinds of capital – productive, commercial and money-dealing capital. Productive capital is invested in the employment of labour-power to produce commodities (which may take the form of services as well as material goods). Workers employed in this process of production are solely responsible for the creation of new value: it is the portion of this value (surplus-value) that is appropriated by capital that is the source of the profits secured by different capitalists. (Strictly speaking, productive capital is a broader category than industrial capital as the latter is conventionally understood, since it includes, for example, the transport of commodities to their point of sale as well as agriculture, but, for ease of exposition, I shall henceforth treat the two as equivalent.) Commercial and money-dealing capitalists are able to secure a share of the surplus-value generated in production thanks to the economic functions they perform. Commercial capitalists are responsible for the circulation of commodities (much of retail, advertising, etc.).

Money-dealing capitalists by contrast operate in what Marx calls the credit system – the financial markets in contemporary parlance – organizing the lending of money to industrial and commercial capitalists in return for interest on the loans. The source of the interest-bearing capital that is lent out is chiefly idle money generated in the course of the circuit through which productive capital expands itself by extracting and realizing surplus-value – for example, profits that have been neither consumed nor reinvested and revenue set side to cover the depreciation of fixed capital that is not yet ready for replacement.[23] As Makoto Itoh and Costas Lapavitsas put it:

the credit system mobilizes the stagnant money generated in the course of capitalist reproduction, transforming it into interest-bearing (loanable) capital and redirects it toward accumulation. In the first instance, the credit system is a mechanism for the internal reallocation of spare funds among industrial and commercial capitalists. By this token, interest payments are a redistribution of surplus-value among capitals, based on the prior generation of idle money by these capitals.[24]

Itoh and Lapavitsas draw out an important implication of this analysis:

For Marx, both commercial and money-dealing capital (or banking capital as the more advanced capitalist form of the latter) are integral parts of the sphere of circulation in the total social capital. They minimize the costs of exchange and do not abandon the circuit as part of their intrinsic movement. As capitals integral to the circuit, they take part in the redistribution of total surplus-value on the same footing as industrial capital. In short, they participate in the formation of the average rate of profit. Interest-bearing capital, on the other hand, is constantly formed out of the circuit, and enters and exits the latter. By so doing, interest-bearing capital mobilizes the spare money funds present in the course of accumulation, and reallocates them among the capitals integral to the circuit . . . Consequently, interest-bearing capital also earns a share of the total surplus-value, but not on the same basis as industrial, commercial and money-dealing (or banking) capital. Interest-bearing capital does not take part in the determination of the average rate of profit, but earns interest instead.[25]

Banks, in other words, are capitalist firms that seek to realize comparable (or superior) profits to those gained by other capitals by specializing in activities in the financial markets, where loanable capital is raised. The return on these activities – the rate of interest – is determined by different factors, above all the supply of and demand for loanable capital, from those responsible for the overall rate of profit (the ratio between total surplus-value and total capital). Given the same rate of interest, improvements in information technology or financial innovations (such as those involved in the development of CDOs) may reduce banks' costs and thereby increase their profitability. This distinction between the *character* of banking capitals (no different from that of other profit-seeking capitalist firms) and the *sphere* in which they are active (the financial markets) admits the possibility that other actors may become involved in this sphere. This possibility has been realized in contemporary financialization. Industrial and commercial firms that derive the bulk of their profits else-where – in, respectively, production and circulation – raise money directly in the financial market, chiefly because it is cheaper for them to do so than acting through the inter-mediary of the banks. There is a tendency for them also to engage in banking activities, as an independent source of profits – as, for example, leading supermarket chains do in Britain and General Electric and General Motors have long done in the US. But, as we shall see further below, banks have also become increasingly active in lending to working-class households, who borrow pri-marily to support their own consumption and must cover the repayments of principal and interest out of their wage-income.[26]

It is appropriate, in the context of discussing this third meaning of financialization, to consider the credit deriva-tives that are massively traded in contemporary financial markets. Derivatives are financial instruments whose mon-etary value derives at least notionally from that of another asset: they originated as a means of hedging against potentially damaging changes in prices by, for example, allowing economic actors to buy the option to purchase commodities at a certain price at some future date. Credit derivatives represent a considerable extension: CDOs are one example. Another – credit default swaps (CDSs), which are a way of taking out insurance against a bor-rower defaulting on a loan – also played a very important role in the development of the financial crisis. According to George Soros, one reason why the decision of the Bush administration to allow Lehman Brothers to go bust in September 2008 proved to be 'a game-changing event, with catastrophic consequences', was that it sharply raised the price of CDSs, in the process forcing a government takeover of the insurance giant AIG, which had gone short on CDSs and therefore faced huge losses additional to those it had already suffered through its role in the CDS market and hence bankruptcy.[27] The fact that an insurance company should blow itself up through its entanglement with abstruse financial products is itself a symptom of financialization.

In a pioneering Marxist study of derivatives, Dick Bryan and Michael Rafferty write, '[t]he central, universal characteristic of derivatives is their capacity to "dismantle" or "unbundle" any asset into constituent attributes and trade those attributes without trading the asset itself'. One might treat this as a symptom of the tendency of capitalism, increasingly unrestricted in the neoliberal era, to commodify everything, even abstract properties. But Bryan and Rafferty argue that derivatives must be understood not merely as signs of commodification and instruments of speculation:

> Each derivative product is a package of conversion of one form of capital to another – whether this be a simple commodity futures contract or a complex conversion of a particular currency index to a particular stock market index. When all these products are taken together, they form a complex of conversions, in which any 'bit' of capital anywhere and with any time profile, can be measured against any other bit of capital.[28]

For Bryan and Rafferty, this quality of derivatives as *'meta-capital* whose distinctive role to bind and blend different sorts of "particular" capital' has allowed them to provide the anchor that the international monetary system has lacked since the US abandoned the gold exchange standard in 1971: 'derivatives permit all forms of capital ("moneys" and "commodities"), at all places and over time, to be commensurate, thereby effectively breaking down the differences between different forms of money (different currencies; different interest rate profiles) and between commodities and money'. Generated by the workings of the financial markets themselves, they provide 'a network of anchors' allowing 'individual capitals to manage their exposure to financial instability and operate "as if" the global financial system were stable'.[29] Consequently derivatives cannot be dismissed as a marginal phenomenon. This is true in terms of scale – according to the Bank for International Settlements, the total notional value of contracts outstanding in over-the-counter (OTC) derivatives (which are not traded in formal exchanges) peaked at $683,700bn in mid-2008, more than eleven times global output.[30] But it is also true of the pervasiveness of resort to derivatives. Thus the spot prices of many commodities are now based on those set in derivatives markets. Meanwhile, according to Bryan and Rafferty, '[f]inancial derivatives are becoming increasingly standard ways that large and even small corporations manage various risks'.[31] But, despite these virtues, 'the global financial system' *wasn't* 'stable'. More than that, derivatives helped to destabilize it. To understand this better, we need to look more closely at the nature of financial crises and their relationship to the broader capitalist system.

Three perspectives on financial crises

So financialization means the greater autonomy of the financial sector, the proliferation of financial institutions and instruments, and the integration of a broad range of economic actors in financial markets. These developments are all the more significant if financial markets are themselves unstable. The greater the weight of finance, the more then would it destabilize the economy as a whole. How, then, are we to understand the nature of financial instability? Here the mainstream neoclassical orthodoxy is of little use, affirming as it does the Efficient Market Hypothesis, which was formulated by George Gibson in 1883: 'when shares become publicly known on an open market, the value which they acquire may be regarded as the judgement of the best intelligence regarding them'.[32] This claim implies that, in a properly working financial market, assets are always correctly priced. So the sudden disastrous fluctuations in asset prices that are characteristic of financial panics can't happen in these conditions. This is, putting it mildly, hard to sustain empirically. As Martin Wolf acknowledges, '[t]he age of financial liberalization was . . . an age of crises'. He cites a study that estimates there were 139 financial crises between 1973 and 1997, twice the level of the era before 1914 that is often described as that of the 'first globalization', of a liberal world economy in which, under British hegemony, money flowed freely across national borders. There were, moreover, a mere thirty-eight financial crises between 1945 and 1971, a period when capitalism was more nationally regulated.[33] These figures, of course, don't include the dotcom crash of 2000 and the financial crisis of 2007–8, both of which originated in the very heart of neoliberal capitalism, in the US itself. If financial markets weren't working properly there, after thirty years of deregulation, they never will.[34]

Let's take a look then at three alternative perspectives on financial crises, Keynesian, classical–liberal and Marxist. Common to the Keynesian and Marxist approaches is an understanding that money matters. This is fundamentally different from the treatment of money both in the classical political economy of David Ricardo and in neoclassical orthodoxy, which is expressed clearly by Joseph Schumpeter:

> money has been called a 'garb' or 'veil' of the things that really matter, both to households and firms and to the

analysts who observe them. Not only *can* it be discarded
whenever we are analysing the fundamental features of the
economic process but it *must* be discarded just as a veil
must be drawn aside if we are to see the face behind it.[35]

Milton Friedman articulates the neoclassical view even
more starkly: 'Despite the importance of enterprises and
money in our actual economy, and despite the numerous
and complex problems they raise, the central characteristic
of the market technique of achieving coordination is fully
displayed in the simple exchange economy that contains
neither enterprises nor money.'[36] In the quantity theory of
money of which Friedman was the most powerful recent
exponent, the stock of money simply determines the abso-
lute level of prices. Paradoxically, the founder of monetarism's main policy prescription was that the state must
ensure the money supply plays the passive role ascribed to
it by his theory, neither contracting dangerously (as Friedman believed had happened during the Great Depression)
or expanding excessively and thereby pushing up the rate
of inflation. Thus, as Hyman Minsky puts it, neoclassical
orthodoxy relies on 'models that abstract from corporate
boardrooms and Wall Street. The model does not deal
with time, money, uncertainty, financing of ownership of
capital assets, and investment.' Hence 'it fails to explain
how a financial crisis can emerge out of the normal functioning of the economy and why the economy of one
period may be susceptible to crisis while that of another
is not'.[37]

Minsky

Minsky's work is the most influential version of the first,
Keynesian perspective on financial crises; his most important book, *Stabilizing an Unstable Economy*, was rushed
back into print soon after the outbreak of the subprime
crisis. Minsky develops the theme of uncertainty as a
chronic feature of the capitalist economy that Keynes

emphasizes in his later writings, as in this letter: 'I should, I think, be prepared to argue that, in a world ruled by uncertainty with an uncertain future linked to an actual present, a final position of equilibrium, such as one deals with in static economics, does not properly exist.'[38] Hence *'the importance of money flows from its being a link between the present and the future'*.[39] Like Marx, Keynes and Minsky see capital accumulation as one of the defining features of a modern capitalist economy. Accumulation implies tying up significant productive resources in a project that, if things go well, will generate returns over a relatively protracted period of time. This amounts to taking a bet on the future, a bet whose chances of success cannot be calculated according to the quantitative models on which investment banks and hedge funds rely. When I estimate the risk of some future event occurring I do so in the belief that I can assign a precise number to the probability of it taking place. An uncertain event is one to which no such quantifiable probability can be assigned. The failure of these models to take into account sufficiently the critical distinction between risk and uncertainty, first drawn explicitly by Frank Knight, helps to explain why they broke down spectacularly as the financial crisis developed.[40] 'We are seeing things that were 25-standard deviation events [i.e. events that are only supposed to happen every 100,000 years or more], several days in a row', David Viniar, chief financial officer of Goldman Sachs, complained in August 2007.[41]

Minsky argues:

Uncertainty is largely a matter of dealing today with a future that by its very nature is highly conjectural. In a world with uncertainty, units make do with and react to the often surprising fruits of past decisions as they ripen. One concrete manifestation of the uncertainty that rules is found in the *willingness* to lever or debt-finance positions in inherited capital assets, financial assets, and newly produced capital assets.[42]

Indeed, for Minsky, the key form of uncertainty thanks to which '*instability is an inherent and inescapable flaw of capitalism*', derives precisely because of the ways in which firms become vulnerable through how they raise money to finance their investments. He distinguishes three forms of finance – hedge finance, where the borrowing can be covered by actual or expected income; speculative finance, where debts aren't paid off but are rolled over; and Ponzi finance, where additional borrowing is needed to cover existing debts. Each form of finance is more vulnerable than the preceding one. Hedge finance turns out badly when expected returns don't actually appear, perhaps because demand for the product proves less favourable, or because the costs of production rise. Speculative finance is vulnerable also to developments specific to the financial markets, for example, higher interest rates or tougher credit ratings. Worse still

> [a] Ponzi unit is not only vulnerable to developments that would affect a speculative unit, but its balance sheet deteriorates as interest or even dividends are paid by increasing debts. Thus, the cash flows that must be earned for the financial conditions to be fulfilled become greater, and the equity–debt ratio on the balance sheet deteriorates. The conditions for full debt validation become stricter, and the shortfall of earnings or the rise in interest costs that makes it highly unlikely that payment commitments will not be fulfilled becomes smaller. Although periods of Ponzi finance may be part of the normal cyclical experience of firms, being forced into Ponzi-financing arrangements by income shortfalls or interest costs escalation is a systemic part of the process that leads to widespread bankruptcy.[43]

Hence: 'The greater the weight of speculative and Ponzi finance, the smaller the overall margins of safety in the economy and the greater the fragility of the financial structure.' Minsky argues that

> in a world of uncertainty, given capital assets with a long gestation period, and the sophisticated financial practices

of Wall Street, the successful functioning of an economy
within an initially robust financial structure will lead to a
structure that becomes more fragile as time elapses. Endogenous forces make a situation dominated by hedge
finance unstable, and endogenous disequilibrating forces
will become greater as the weight of speculative and
Ponzi finance increases.[44]

The most important of these 'endogenous disequilibrating
forces' are the banks. Money is created when banks make
loans and destroyed when the loans are repaid. Banks lend
out far in excess of their capital (equity); hence the importance of their leverage, the ratio of assets (loans) to equity.
'A bank that increases leverage without adversely affecting
profits per dollar of assets increases its profitability.' Hence
banks have an incentive to come up with financial innovations that allow them profitably to increase their leverage
but that may draw their borrowers deeper into forms of
speculative and Ponzi finance. The result, over the course
of the business cycle, is a tendency for economic expansions to develop into uncontrollable booms, as an increasing proportion of investment is based on the expectation
of continuing rises in the price of different financial assets,
and then to bust, usually when interest rates go up to a
level that destabilizes firms reliant on speculative and Ponzi
finance. Hence, *pace* Alan Greenspan, 'in a world with
capitalist finance it is simply not true that the pursuit
of each unit of its own self-interest will lead an economy
to equilibrium. The self-interest of bankers, levered investors, and investment producers can lead the economy
to inflationary expansions and unemployment-creating
contractions.'[45]

Minsky thinks it unlikely that this cycle will lead to
what, in a famous essay, he calls 'It' – the Great Depression
– happening again. This is because of the role of 'Big Government'. In the first place, the relative weight of state
expenditure in a contemporary capitalist economy means
that the tendency for recessions to produce or increase a

budget deficit, as tax revenues fall and welfare spending rises, serves to counteract the contraction of effective demand and thereby to sustain the finances of firms and households. Secondly, central banks such as the US Federal Reserve Board act as a lender of last resort and thereby stabilize financial markets and asset values. But these activities come at a price. The injections of money into the economy that they involve help to explain why, since the Second World War, there has been a positive, and sometimes accelerating rate of inflation. Moreover:

> Federal Reserve lender-of-last-resort actions, directly or indirectly, set floors under the prices of assets or ceilings on financing terms, thus socializing some of the risks involved in speculative finance. But such socialization of risks in financial markets encourages risk-taking in financing positions in capital assets, which, in turn, increases the potential for instability when carried out for an extended period.[46]

Moreover, Minsky seems to think there is a cycle in financial regulation. After a major and catastrophic crash, such as that of 1929, tight restrictions are imposed on the financial markets. But, over time, these restrictions are eroded, particularly as banks come up with new financial instruments, responding especially to the demands for extra finance in conditions of economic expansion. And so, while the state can both counteract and rein in the excesses of capitalism, Minsky writes in the concluding sentence of his book, 'instability, put to rest by one set of reforms will, after time, emerge in a new guise'. He appears less optimistic than Keynes about the feasibility of permanently putting a state-managed capitalism onto the path of prosperity, as is reflected in his 'financial instability hypothesis':

1. Capitalist market mechanisms cannot lead to a sustained, stable-price, full-employment equilibrium.
2. Serious business cycles are due to financial attributes that are essential to capitalism.[47]

Minsky offers an extremely valuable analysis, particularly because he is so attentive to the specific properties and mechanisms of capitalist finance. Its relevance to the contemporary crisis should be obvious. But he shares with Keynes a fundamental ambiguity about how deeply rooted the problem of capitalist instability lies. Keynes famously argues that 'a somewhat comprehensive socialization of investment will prove the only means of securing an approximation to full employment'. He also proposes that these measures could be introduced piecemeal, and should stop well short of 'a system of State Socialism which would embrace most of the economic life of the community'.[48] But how, particularly given the emphasis that Keynes puts on capital accumulation, this key activity could be socialized without subverting capitalist economic relations more generally is left quite unclear. Similarly, Minsky worries about the effects of regulating financial markets on the viability of capitalism itself:

> Federal Reserve policy therefore needs to continuously 'lean against' the use of speculative and Ponzi finance. But Ponzi finance is a usual way of debt-financing investment in process in a capitalist society. Consequently capitalism without financial practices that lead to instability may be less innovative and expansionary; lessening the possibility of disaster might very well take part of the spark of creativity out of the capitalist system.[49]

This suggests the importance of seeking to explore more deeply than Minsky does the relationship between capitalist economic relations as a whole and the financial markets.

Hayek

Oddly enough, one way of going deeper is offered in the most unexpected of places, in the classical–liberal analysis of the relationship between investment and credit offered by F. A. von Hayek that forms the second perspective on financial crises that I want to consider here. Hayek enjoyed the good fortune (from his perspective) of living long enough to see the eclipse of classical liberalism in the Keynesian era reversed with the triumph of neoliberalism in the 1970s and 1980s. It is, however, in an early work, *Prices and Production*, first published in 1931, as the Great Depression was just getting into its stride, that I am interested here. One striking feature of this work is that Hayek rejects the neoclassical orthodoxy that money doesn't matter. Thus he writes at the end of the book: 'I hope to have shown that, under existing conditions, money will always exert a determining influence on the course of economic events and that, therefore, no analysis of actual economic phenomena is complete if the role played by money is neglected.'[50]

But Hayek's treatment of money and credit comes in the context of an analysis (which derives from the Austrian school of neoclassical economists headed by Eugen von Böhm-Bawerk), of capitalist production and, more specifically, of the tendency for the structure of production to become more roundabout. That is, it shifts over time towards the production of what Marx would call the means of production, but which Hayek describes as 'intermediate products': 'it is an essential feature of our modern "capitalistic" system of production that any moment a far larger proportion of the available means of production is employed to provide consumers' goods for some more or less distant future than is used for the satisfaction of immediate needs'. The critical issue for Hayek is how the shift to more roundabout processes of production is financed:

> a transition to more (or less) capitalistic methods of production will take place if the total demand for producers' goods (expressed in money) increases (or decreases) relatively to the demand for consumers' goods. This may come about in one of two ways: either as a result of changes in the volume of voluntary saving (or its opposite) or as a

result of a change in the quantity of money which alters the funds at the disposal of the entrepreneurs for the purchase of producers' goods.[51]

In the first case, where the distribution of demand changes as a result of 'voluntary decisions on the part of individuals' to save, the change in the structure of production is sustainable. Not so in the second case, where the change is 'caused by the granting of additional credits to producers'. Here again,

> the use of a larger proportion of the means of production for the manufacture of intermediate products can only be brought about by a retrenchment of consumption. But now this sacrifice is not voluntary, and is not made by those who will reap the benefit from the new investments. It is made by consumers in general who, because of the increased competition from the entrepreneurs who have received the additional money, are forced to forego part of what they used to consume. It comes about not because they want to consume less, but because they get less goods for their money income. There can be no doubt that, if their money receipts were to rise again, they would immediately attempt to expand consumption in the usual proportion . . . then at once the money stream will be redistributed between consumers and producers according to the wishes of the individuals concerned, and the artificial distribution, due to the injection of the new money, will, partly, at any rate, be reversed . . . That is to say, production will become less capitalistic and that part of the new capital which was sunk into equipment adapted only to the more capitalistic processes will be lost.[52]

Naturally, those capitalists who face the prospect of their investments being written off will resist. The result will be a push-and-pull between capitalists and consumers, reflected in shifts in the relative prices of producer and consumer goods. To the extent that the banks continue to advance more credit to capitalists (and the extra profits offered by the rise in the relative price of consumer goods will give the latter an incentive to borrow and the former the incentive to lend), 'it will therefore be possible to continue the prolonged methods of production or perhaps even to extend them still further'. But this process of credit-driven expansion eventually becomes unsustainable, if only because of the 'rapid and continuous rise in prices' it generates. Trying to avoid a recession by injecting yet more credit will simply postpone the real solution, which lies 'in the most speedy and complete adaptation possible of the structure of production to the proportion between the demand for consumers' goods and the demand for producers' goods as determined by voluntary saving and spending'. Hayek's conclusion is to reaffirm 'the old truth that we may perhaps prevent a crisis by checking expansion in time, but that we can do nothing to get out of it before its natural end, once it has come'.[53]

So, like Keynes and Minsky, Hayek believes that the credit system generates destabilizing booms. Unlike them, he thinks the state should do nothing to prevent the bust, apart from moderating the expansion of credit. Hayek's underlying commitment to the same kind of free-market framework that Friedman would later develop is signalled by the distinction he consistently draws between 'natural' changes in the distribution of demand caused by voluntary decisions to save and 'artificial' changes driven by the expansion of credit. Nevertheless, his analysis is distinctive in the way in which he seeks to relate the destabilizing role of finance to the tendency for production to become more 'capitalistic'. In a compelling contemporary Marxist critique John Strachey points out that in this respect Hayek had stumbled onto the major premiss of Marx's own theory of capitalist crisis.[54]

Harvey

As we have already seen, Marx believes that capitalism is driven by a process of competitive accumulation. Individual capitals seek to realize super-profits by investing in technological innovations that will reduce their costs of production below the average and thereby allow them to undercut their competitors. Other things being equal, the effect will be to increase the organic composition of capital, in other words, the ratio between constant capital, which is invested in the means of production, and variable capital, which is advanced to employ wage-labourers to operate these means of production and thereby to produce commodities. Production, to put it in Hayek's terms, becomes more roundabout. But this tendency for the organic composition of capital to rise is problematic for the process of production itself. The reason why variable capital has this name is because, according to the labour theory of value, only labour can create new value. More specifically, profits derive from the surplus-value that capital appropriates thanks to its control over the means and hence over the process of production. A rising organic composition of capital means that total investment is rising more rapidly than the variable portion devoted to employing wage-labour. Hence the rate of profit – the ratio of surplus-value to the total capital (variable plus constant capital) – falls. There is, Marx emphasizes, only a *tendency* for the rate of profit to fall because of the existence of powerful counter-tendencies. If, for example, the rate of exploitation rises, thereby increasing the total amount of surplus-value, or if capital is reduced in value or price or some of it is physically destroyed, then the effect of a rising organic composition of capital will be partially or wholly counteracted and the rate of profit will not fall or may even rise. This argument underlines that economic crises represent for Marx, not the final breakdown of capitalism, but episodes that are to some degree functional to the system. Higher unemployment makes it easier to force up the rate of exploitation, while bankruptcies represent the destruction of capital, increasing the profitable opportunities for the surviving firms. Hence crises unleash forces that permit a restoration of profitability and growth.[55]

Marxist political economy offers the possibility of integrating this analysis, which is rooted in a theory of the contradictions inherent in the capitalist production process, with one of the added instabilities introduced by financial markets. Marx himself pays considerable attention to money and credit. Value for him is inherently a monetary relation. Money is the universal equivalent, the commodity that takes on the function of representing the value of all the commodities and thereby makes them mutually commensurable. It is by virtue of this that money is able to perform its other functions as, for example, as measure of value, means of exchange and means of payment (this last predominates in the credit system). Capital reaches its purest form in the shape of money – interest-bearing capital, as the drive to expand capital apparently without the intermediary of production. In fact, the various kinds of asset traded on financial markets – stocks, bonds, today different sorts of derivative, and so on – are what Marx calls 'fictitious capital', since they constitute, not actual investments in the production of commodities and extraction of surplus-value, but rather claims on that surplus-value:

> The shares in railways, mining, shipping companies, etc., represent real capital, that is, capital invested and functioning in such enterprises, or the amount of money advanced by stockholders for the purpose of being used as capital in these enterprises . . . But the capital does not exist twice over, once as the capital value of the ownership titles, the shares, and then again as the capital actually invested or to be invested in the enterprise in question. It exists only in the latter form, and the share is nothing but an ownership title, *pro rata*, to the surplus-value which this capital is to realize.[56]

Marx pays close attention to the financial scams and panics of Victorian Britain. His overall view of financial markets is that they simultaneously allow the process of capital accumulation to transcend its limits only to bring it up all the more forcibly against these limits:

If the credit system appears as the principal lever of over-production and excessive speculation in commerce, this is simply because the reproduction process, which is elastic by nature, is now forced to its most extreme limit; and this is because a great part of the social capital is applied by those who are not its owners and who therefore proceed quite unlike owners who, when they function themselves, anxiously weigh the limits of their private capital. This only goes to show how the valorization of capital founded on the antithetical character of capitalist production permits actual free development only up to a certain point, which is constantly broken by the credit system. The credit system hence accelerates the material development of the productive forces and the creation of the world market . . . At the same time, credit accelerates the violent outbreaks of this contradiction, crises, and with these the elements of dissolution of the old mode of production.[57]

As a broad assessment of the credit boom and bust of the past decade, this has a lot to commend it.

The contemporary Marxist work that has most success-fully articulated together the different aspects of Marx's own analysis is David Harvey's *The Limits to Capital*, which has now deservedly attained the status of a classic. Harvey argues that 'Marx meant his exposition of the law of falling profits as a "first-cut" statement of his theory of crisis-formation under capitalism'; Harvey offers a looser reading of the law than Marx, simply positing a general capitalist tendency towards overaccumulation. Through a critical reading of *Capital*, he seeks to develop 'a "second-cut" theory of crisis' that offers 'a more integrated view of the relations between financial phenomena and the dynamics of production'. His overall view of finance is similar to Marx's:

On the surface, at least, the credit system contains the *potential* to straddle the antagonisms between production and consumption, between production and realization, between present uses and future labour, between production and distribution. It also provides means to arbitrate between the individual and class interests of capitalists and so contain the forces making for crises.[58]

But:

the use of credit tends to make matters worse in the long run because it can deal only with problems that arise in exchange and never with those in production. And there are, besides, a whole host of circumstances in which credit can generate price signals to producers and so aggravate the tendencies towards disproportionality and overaccumulation.[59]

One of the most interesting aspects of Harvey's discussion of money and credit lies in the emphasis he lays on what he calls 'the central contradiction between money as measure of value and money as a medium of exchange'. The thought is that the demand, constantly generated by the accumulation process, for forms of money that will facilitate the rapid and profitable expansion of economic transactions, will tend to undermine money's function, rooted in its nature as the universal equivalent, to render values mutually commensurable, which in turn is dependent on confidence in its stability and reliability:

we can best interpret the different forms money takes – the money commodity, coins, convertible and inconvertible paper currencies, various credit moneys, etc. – as an outcome of a drive to perfect money as a frictionless, costless and instantaneously adjustable lubricant of exchange while preserving the 'quality' of the money as a measure of value. The uncertain and 'lawless' character of commodity production and exchange leads different economic agents to demand different kinds of money for definite purposes at particular conjunctures. In times of crisis, for example, economic agents typically look to secure forms of money (such as gold), but when commodity production is booming and exchange relations proliferating the demand for credit moneys is bound to rise.[60]

Harvey also offers a punchier version of the same contradiction:

A tension exists, then, between the need to sustain accumulation through credit creation and the need to preserve the quality of money. If the former is inhibited, we end up with an overaccumulation of commodities and devaluation [i.e. recession]. If the quality of money is allowed to go to the dogs, we have generalized devaluation [inflation]. Thus are the dilemmas of modern times neatly presented.[61]

Writing at the start of the 1980s, Harvey no doubt was thinking about the distinctive form of economic crisis that developed at the end of the 1960s, which was characterized by stagflation – that is, the malign combination of accelerating inflation and mass unemployment. But his analysis is suggestive when we seek to consider the origins of the present global economic and financial crisis. As we have seen, Bryan and Rafferty argue that the explosion of financial derivatives in recent decades is in part driven by the need of capitals, in a world monetary system that, since the US went off gold in 1971, is no longer anchored in a commodity form of money, to be able to render different values mutually commensurable. In this respect, and also thanks to the more specific functions of derivatives in facilitating insurance against risk, speculation and (in the case of the banks and shadow banks) an enormous expansion of leverage, they certainly acted, in Harvey's felicitous phrase, as 'a frictionless, costless and instantaneously adjustable lubricant of exchange'. But they have also proved to be a very powerful destabilizing force 'aggravat[ing] the tendencies towards disproportionality and overaccumulation' and generating a flight to 'quality' that has rendered many derivatives worthless. But properly to understand what happened we need to bring together the contradictions of production and finance at work in the credit boom and bust.

More than just a financial crisis

What started as the subprime crisis and then became the credit crunch has morphed into something that extends well beyond the financial markets, as it has generated a world economic slump. The IMF predicted in April 2009 that global gross domestic product would fall by 1.3 per cent that year: 'By any measure, this downturn represents by far the deepest global recession since the Great Depression.' Moreover, '[e]ven once the crisis is over, there will be a difficult transition period, with output growth appreciably below rates seen in the recent past.'[62] But if, plainly, the *effects* of the crisis have spread deep into the 'real' economy, what about its *causes*? Just because it began in the financial system doesn't mean that it was generated there. In the spirit of Marx and Harvey, I argue that what we are confronted with is an economic crisis that exposes the depths of the contradictions that have been at work in the entire process of capital accumulation and not merely, as Keynes and Minsky would contend, the dysfunctions of the financial markets. Making this argument requires, as Harvey suggests, 'a more integrated view of the relations between financial phenomena and the dynamics of production'.[63] A comprehensive analysis of the present crisis requires us to distinguish the following dimensions: (i) a long-term crisis of overaccumulation and profitability; (ii) a global financial system that is both chronically unstable and structurally unbalanced; and (iii) a growing reliance on credit bubbles to sustain economic expansion. Let's explore these dimensions in turn.

A long-term crisis of overaccumulation and profitability

The research of Robert Brenner has demonstrated that the advanced capitalist economies have suffered from relatively low rates of profit since the end of the 1960s. Table

1.1 gives comprehensive figures for the United States, but Japan and Germany show a broadly similar pattern.[64] The result has been a significant decline in the rate of economic growth of all the three main centres of advanced capitalism – North America, Western Europe and Japan – by comparison with the Long Boom of the 1950s and 1960s. This slowdown is clear in Table 1.2, which also demonstrates that the high rate of growth that Asia outside Japan has been able to sustain throughout the postwar era has not

Table 1.1 US Non-Financial Corporate Net Profit Rate by Business Cycle, 1948–2007

1948–1959	0.1327
1959–1969	0.1459
1969–1973	0.1137
1969–1979	0.1048
1979–1990	0.0979
1990–2000	0.1081
2000–2007	0.0951

Source: R. Brenner, Paper for *Historical Materialism* Conference, 11 November 2007, corrected and updated

Table 1.2 Global GDP growth rates 1820–2003 (annual average compound growth rates)

	1820–70	1870–1913	1913–50	1950–73	1973–2003
Western Europe	1.68	2.11	1.19	4.79	2.19
USA	4.20	3.94	2.84	3.93	2.94
Japan	0.41	2.44	2.21	9.29	2.62
Asia (excl. Japan)	0.04	0.98	0.82	5.13	5.71
World	0.94	2.12	1.82	4.90	3.17

Source: A. Maddison, *Contours of the World Economy, 1–2030 AD* (Oxford, 2007), Table A5, p. 380

been sufficient to offset the effect of slow growth in the core zones.

David McNally argues, in effect, that this kind of interpretation of the entire period since 1973 is misleading, in part because it is characterized as one of crises by reference to the Long Boom:

> the unique quarter-century long postwar boom (1949–73) ought not to be the benchmark against which everything else is deemed a 'crisis'. That great boom was the product of an exceptional set of social-historical circumstances that triggered an unprecedented wave of expansion. But, prolonged expansion with rising levels of output, wages and employment in the core economies is not the capitalist norm; and the absence of all of these is not invariably a 'crisis'.[65]

McNally is right that the period 1949–73 is an exceptional one in the history of capitalism, as Table 1.2 shows. This isn't just because the rates of growth both globally and in all the major regions (with the rather significant exception of the US) were historically unprecedented; this expansion was also not interrupted by serious recessions. This distinguishes it from the period before the First World War, when the average growth rate in the US was just as robust, but the expansion was punctuated by severe economic slumps, notably in the mid-1870s and mid-1890s and after the 1907 crash. Any serious political economy has to explain why global capitalism was able to achieve such high, sustained and stable growth. In my view, the critical factor is provided by what Michael Kidron called the permanent arms economy: the very high levels of military expenditure that both the US and the Soviet Union maintained at the height of the Cold War in the 1950s and 1960s offset the tendency for the organic composition of capital to rise and thereby kept profitability high until the Nixon administration slashed arms spending at the end of the 1960s.[66]

Any serious political economy has also to explain why capitalism has been unable to keep up the high, sustained and stable growth of the 1950s and 1960s. In this respect, the Long Boom is unavoidably 'a benchmark', and the subsequent period is evidently different from it, not simply because of the slowdown in growth rates but because, before the present crisis, it was punctuated by three major global recessions, in the mid-1970s, the early 1980s and the early 1990s. (One might indeed argue that the collapse of the dotcom boom in 2000 marked an aborted fourth recession, for reasons that will become clear below.) The occurrence of these major disruptions is not merely an artefact of Marxist economic catastrophism. The eminently respectable Keynesian economist Christopher Dow, in a study of major recessions, largely, though not exclusively, in Britain in the last three quarters of the twentieth century, notes that 'the contrasts [in rates of growth and unemployment] between these three phases were due mainly to there having been large recessions in the first and third quarter century, but none in the second'. Defining major recessions as occasions when the rate of output growth falls by more than the capacity rate of growth required to keep unemployment constant, and hence output falls absolutely, Dow identifies five major British recessions – 1920–1, 1929–32, 1973–5, 1979–82 and 1989–93.[6]

To describe the period since 1973 as one of crises is not to portray it as one of permanent stagnation. What we have seen has been a partial return to capitalist 'normality', to the sharp oscillations of boom and slump typical of industrial capitalism from the end of the Napoleonic Wars till the late 1940s (though high levels of state expenditure helped to prevent, till 2008–9, the very sharp falls in output typical of pre-war slowdowns). The recessions of the past forty years have been accompanied by phases of significant economic expansion – in Britain, for example, in the mid-1980s and from the mid-1990s to the great bust of 2007–8. Brenner's main study of the crisis of profitability is called *The Economics of Global Turbulence*. This is in many ways an apt characterization, but it's worth recalling that Alan Greenspan named his autobiography *The Age of Turbulence*. Greenspan offers a rather banal discussion of how 'the dynamic that defines capitalism, that of unforgiving market competition, clashes with the human desire for stability and certainty'.[68] It's important to insist that the global economic turbulence after 1973 has not been about this kind of anthropological conflict or even simply the ups and downs of the business cycle. Rather what we have seen are chronic patterns of economic and financial instability reflecting the failure of capital to overcome the underlying crisis of overaccumulation and profitability.

To resolve such a crisis would mean both forcing up the rate of exploitation – getting workers to accept lower wages, longer hours and worse working conditions – and eliminating relatively unprofitable capital, if not through the destruction of the physical assets it represents, then through the reduction of their monetary value. The effects of these processes would be both to increase the mass of profits and to reduce the amount of capital, thereby causing the rate of profit to rise. They imply considerable restructuring and reorganization of capital.[69] To a larger extent, neoliberalism represents the political and ideological framework in which such restructuring has occurred. Though prefigured earlier, the turning point came in 1979, with the coming to office of the Conservatives under Margaret Thatcher in Britain and what Duménil and Lévy slightly melodramatically call the 'coup' that led to a sharp increase in real interest rates, in particular thanks to the monetary squeeze imposed by Paul Volcker, Chairman of the Federal Reserve Board, that October.[70]

The immediate focus of the policy shift was to force down inflation rates, but it reflected a broader disillusionment among American and British policy elites with Keynesian demand management and a feeling that, after the social explosions and shop-floor insurgency of the late

1960s and early 1970s, organized labour was out of control. The resulting move to the right was reinforced by Ronald Reagan's victory in the 1980 presidential election. The interest rate hike and the associated rise in the exchange rates of the dollar and the pound sterling had a profound global impact. Externally, Third World states that had been encouraged by Western banks to borrow during the 1970s were confronted with soaring debts and interest payments. The resulting defaults created favourable conditions for the export of neoliberal policies as a condition for the 'rescue' packages assembled by the IMF; the Washington Consensus began to crystallize. Domestically, the turn to neoliberalism, amid the global recession of 1979–82, helped to force a dramatic contraction and reorganization especially of manufacturing industry involving major confrontations with powerful groups of organized workers, who suffered a series of devastating defeats. In Britain this culminated in the great miners' strike of 1984–5. In the US, what Brenner calls 'wage-repression' became endemic:

> Between 1979 and 1990, real hourly compensation in the private business economy grew at an average annual rate of 0.1 per cent. The trend in these years for hourly real wages and salaries alone (excluding benefits) for production and non-supervisory workers was worse, *falling* at an average annual rate of 1 per cent. At no time previously in the twentieth century had real wage growth been anywhere near so slow for anywhere near so long.[71]

The result of this harsh squeeze and the broader process of restructuring of which it was part was a significant recovery of profitability from the early 1980s that was associated with a revival in the competiveness of US-based capitals – under heavy pressure from their rivals in Japan and West Germany from the 1960s onwards. What was involved was a sustained increase in the rate of exploitation. According to Simon Mohun, 'the value of labour power fell every year [after 1979] . . . (apart from a small rise in the first half of the 1990s and again in 2000–01)'. This reflected more than the wage repression stressed by Brenner, since Mohun defines the value of labour-power as the ratio of the real wage to labour productivity. It fell because '[p]roductivity growth resumed after 1980, but the real hourly wage rate showed no growth at all for two decades'.[72] In other words, the fruits of higher productivity went to capital. Mohun has also shown that the technical composition of capital, the physical correlate of the organic composition of capital, rose steadily in the 1960s and 1970s, but stagnated or even fell in the subsequent two decades. If this is correct, then the huge expansion of credit in recent decades has not, as Hayek argued it would, enabled production to become more roundabout. Mohun suggests the increase in labour productivity that took place during the 1980s and 1990s in the absence of capital deepening may have resulted from reorganizations of the labour-process reflecting a balance of class forces that was much more favourable to capital.[73]

But, despite the squeeze on productivity and real wages, the rate of profit did not return to the levels of the 1950s and 1960s. In their own careful empirical study of the US rate of profit (which seems to contradict their argument that global capitalism has overcome the structural crisis of the 1970s), Duménil and Lévy write: 'Overall, the value of the profit rate in 2000 is still only half of its value of 1948, and between 60 and 75% of its average value for the decade 1956–1965.'[74] As Figure 1.2 shows, 1997 proved to be a turning point, since the recovery in US profitability peaked then, and thereafter went partially into reverse. According to Mohun, 'the rate of profit in the US economy halved between 1965 and 1982, recovered to about its 1973 level by 1997, and thereafter fell sharply to approach its 1979–83 levels by 2001'.[75]

As we saw above, there are two ways of increasing the rate of profit – exploiting workers more and devaluing capital. The implication of the fact that profitability was not restored to the levels of the 1950s and 1960s, despite

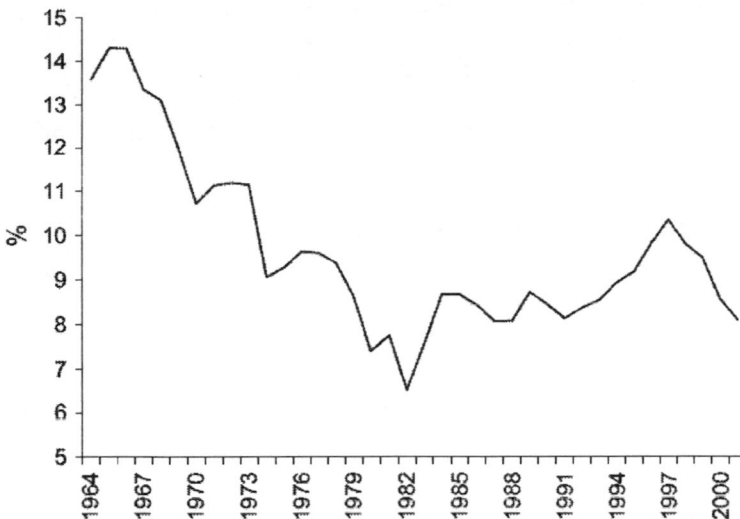

Figure 1.2   The pre-tax average rate of profit, US, 1964–2001
Source: S. Mohun, 'Distributive Shares in the US Economy,
1964–2001', *Cambridge Journal of Economics*, 30 (2006), Fig. 1,
p. 348

the increase in the rate of exploitation, is that there was
too much capital to be profitably employed. Harvey writes:
'Devaluation is the underside to overaccumulation.'[76] To
put it another way, if not enough capital is devalued,
through bankruptcies, write-offs and the like, the result is
continuing overaccumulation. Writing during the early
stages of the Great Depression, the Marxist economist
Evgeny Preobrazhensky suggested that, as the accumulation of capital leads to what he calls 'monopolism', huge
reserves of fixed capital tend to build up, blocking economic recovery from recession.[77] Harvey addresses the
problem in what he calls his ' "third-cut" theory', which
seeks 'to integrate the geography of uneven development
into the theory of crisis' and is concerned with how capital
seeks to displace crisis through a 'spatial fix', by finding
new locations for investment:

The more open the world is to geographical restructuring, the more easily temporary resolutions to problems of over-accumulation can be found . . . Crises are reduced to minor switching crises as flows of capital and labour switch from one region to another, or even reverse themselves, and spark regional devaluations (which can sometimes be intense) as well as major adjustments in the spatial structures (such as the transport system) designed to facilitate spatial flows.[78]

The spatial fix is, however, only temporary as the capital sunk into new geographical locations itself becomes an obstacle to further expansion:

The circulation of capital is increasingly imprisoned within immobile physical and social infrastructures which are crafted to support certain kinds of production, certain kinds of labour process, distributional arrangements, consumption patterns, and so on. Increasing quantities of fixed capital and longer turnover times on production check uninhibited mobility. The growth of productive forces, in short, acts as a barrier to rapid geographical restructuring in exactly the same way as it hinders the dynamic of future accumulation by the imposition of the dead weight of past investments.[79]

Undoubtedly the world economy has experienced very significant spatial reorganization in the past generation. The most important development has been the emergence of East Asia as the most dynamic zone of global capitalism – first as Japan was joined in the 1970s and 1980s by the 'Four Tigers' (South Korea, Taiwan, Hong Kong and Singapore) as new centres of capital accumulation, and then, more recently, with China's rise as a major platform for the production and export of manufactured goods. Many see the rise of Asia, and above all China, as capitalism's salvation. McNally offers a qualified version of this kind of view from a Marxist perspective. He insists, entirely correctly, that 'we need to treat the world economy as a totality that is more than the sum of its parts', and criticizes Brenner for treating the advanced capitalist states as a proxy for this whole. On that basis McNally contends that 'intense processes of capitalist restructuring throughout the neoliberal period created a new social-spatial reconfiguration of capital and a new, uneven and volatile wave of capitalist expansion', above all in East Asia, which, '[b]y the 1990s, . . . had become the centre of a new burst of world accumulation' thanks in particular to the prodigious growth in the global industrial workforce force that it contributed.[80]

The significance of this restructuring, and the redistribution of global economic power that it represents, is undeniable. I return to its geopolitical implications in Chapter 2. But whether East Asian expansion was sufficient to bring to a close the era of crises that began at the beginning of the 1970s is quite another matter. To say that it was 'uneven and volatile' is an understatement. During the recovery of the mid-to-late 1980s Japan and the Tiger economies grew spectacularly, and the penetration of the US by Japanese capital and exports became a major political issue, creating considerable tensions between Tokyo and Washington. But the Japanese boom facilitated the development of a speculative 'bubble economy' centred on soaring real-estates prices whose collapse at the beginning of the 1990s left Japan caught in a protracted deflationary recession. What Brenner calls the 'Reverse Plaza Accord' – the decision of the Clinton administration in 1995 to allow the dollar to rise against other major currencies – was intended, by promoting a fall in the yen, to stimulate Japan's exports and thereby to revive its economy. But the yen's fall against the dollar (by 60 per cent between April 1995 and April 1997) crucified the smaller East Asian economies, which had pegged their currencies to the dollar and so found their exports undercut by cheaper Japanese goods. This was a crucial underlying cause of the East Asian crisis of 1997–8, which was precipitated by a flight of capital from the

Table 1.3 Five biggest economies' share of world GDP, 1980–2008 (%, market exchange rates)

Year	UK	Germany	China	Japan	United States
1980	4.61	7.02	2.6	9.00	23.7
1990	4.46	6.78	1.7	13.28	25.4
1995	3.91	8.52	2.4	17.81	27.0
2000	4.63	5.96	3.8	14.72	30.73
2005	5.4	6.2	5.0	10.11	27.55
2007	5.11	6.05	6.2	7.99	25.17
2008	4.41	6.04	7.25	8.11	23.5

Source: International Monetary Fund, *World Economic Outlook Database*, www.imf.org

region as investors woke up to the deteriorating economic situation.[81]

Critical to economic recovery in both Japan and the rest of East Asia was the Chinese economic boom, which offered a market for its neighbours' complex industrial goods (and encouraged them to relocate some of their productive capacity to cheaper Chinese sites). But it is important not to read back China's impact into earlier decades. Table 1.3 shows how China's share of global GDP has risen over the past thirty years with increasing speed. But it is only during the 2000s that it became sufficiently large to have a significant impact on the world economy. And even now the size of the Chinese economy must be seen in proportion: it remains between a quarter and a third the size of the US economy, which has fluctuated over the past generation around 25 per cent of global output. The *relationship* between China and the US has undoubtedly reshaped the world economy since in the collapse of the dotcom boom in 2000. Properly to understand this relationship requires us to look more closely at how the role of finance has changed in recent decades.

An unstable and unbalanced global financial system

The re-emergence of globally integrated financial markets characterized by a high degree of international capital mobility was a process that took several decades. The first real break in the managed financial system of the early postwar years – in which currencies were fixed against the dollar, which itself was anchored in gold, and states exercised their right under the 1944 Bretton Woods agreements setting up the system to impose restrictions on international capital movements – came at the beginning of the 1960s. The emergence of the Eurodollar market allowed currencies to be traded beyond the borders of their issuing states. But the increasing power of financial markets was demonstrated by the prolonged crisis of the pound sterling from the late 1950s onwards and by the growing monetary instability surrounding the dollar that eventually led the Nixon administration to break the link with gold in August 1971. The agents of this transformation included private actors – for example, transnational corporations seeking to protect their profits from currency instability, and banks looking for new sources of income as industrial and commercial firms became less reliant on them for finance. But states – particularly the US and Britain – became critical forces driving financial liberalization. As a new neoliberal economic policy regime began to take shape in the mid-1970s, a series of decisive changes were initiated – the abolition of fixed commissions for US stock trades in May 1975; the scrapping of exchange controls by the Thatcher government in September 1979; the 'Volcker shock' that October; the 1986 Big Bang that opened the City of London to the more intense competition that Wall Street had experienced since the 1975 reform; the final repeal of the Glass-Steagall Act separating investment and commercial banks in 1999; and the US Commodity Futures Modernization Act 2000, which protected the explosively growing derivatives market from tight regulation.[82]

This dramatic policy shift was prompted in part by effective lobbying by financial institutions with an interest in the changes but more importantly by the broader ideologico-political transformation involved in the triumph of neoliberalism. One of the main consequences sought through this transformation – the subjection of national economies to the discipline of global financial markets – was certainly achieved. But it is also important to grasp the geopolitical significance of financial liberalization. The break with gold did not represent the abandonment of US global financial hegemony. On the contrary, confronted with an increasingly powerful challenge to US manufacturing firms from rivals in Japan and West Germany, the Nixon administration developed a new strategy based on exploiting the dollar's position as the main international reserve currency in a world of floating exchange rates both to maintain the competitiveness of American firms and entrench US financial supremacy. As Eric Helleiner puts it,

administration officials realized that a more open, liberal international financial order would help preserve US policy autonomy in the face of growing external and internal deficits. In the short run, they perceived speculative capital movements as an important central tool in the US strategy of encouraging foreigners to absorb the adjustment burden required to correct the country's large current account deficits . . . [In the longer term,] it was clear that a non-negotiated, market-oriented system would preserve America's dominant position in international finance. The dollar's position as a world currency, for example, would be preserved and reinforced in an open financial system because US financial markets and the Eurodollar market would still be the most attractive international market for private and public investors. No such markets existed to make the yen or the deutsche mark as attractive a reserve currency to hold because the Japanese and German financial markets were underdeveloped and overregulated. The unique depth and liquidity of US financial markets also ensure that private investors, if given the freedom to invest globally, would continue to underwrite US deficits through their holdings of attractive US assets.[83]

What Peter Gowan has called 'the Dollar Wall-Street Regime' allowed the US to respond to recessions and balance of payment deficits with aggressive bouts of dollar devaluation intended to restore the competiveness of American firms – in the early and late 1970s, the mid-1980s and the early and mid-2000s.[84] It also, as Helleiner notes, made it possible for Washington to finance a chronic balance of payments deficit, which had reached around 6 per cent of national income by the mid-2000s. Martin Wolf provides an illuminating analysis of how this worked in the lead-up to the present crisis. He points to the 'puzzles' that, at the height of the credit boom, real interest rates were very low, despite the huge US balance of payments deficit, which should, in the normal course of things, have pushed global interest rates up because of the American need to borrow abroad. What made this state of affairs possible, Wolf argues, is that a global 'savings glut' has developed. More precisely, several key regions – China and the rest of 'developing Asia', Japan, the oil-exporting countries and the euro-zone have been running a surplus of savings over investments. In the US the reverse is true, reflecting growing government borrowing and a very low level of savings by households. As a result, '[t]he United States has been absorbing about 70 percent of the surplus savings of the rest of the world'.[85]

The key element in this story is provided by the East Asian economies – Japan, South Korea, Taiwan and, above all, China. The lesson these countries' rulers drew from the crisis of the late 1990s is that they must never allow themselves to run up big balance of payments deficits and thereby to become vulnerable to the kind of rapid inflows and outflows of foreign capital that proved so destructive then. So they have pursued managed exchange-rate policies whose aim is to prevent their currencies from rising too far against the US dollar and hence to keep their exports relatively cheap. One consequence of this policy was that the East Asian states had to buy foreign currencies (above all dollars) to prevent their own from rising, accumulating, from the millennium onwards, vast foreign exchange reserves: 'By March 2007 the total global stock of foreign-currency reserves had reached $5.3 trillion. China alone had $1.2 trillion and Japan had another $890 billion. Both Taiwan and South Korea held more reserves than the entire euro-zone. Asia held $3.3 trillion dollars in all – just three fifths of the global total.'[86]

Much of this money was then lent back to the US, allowing it to finance its balance of payments deficit. Some economists have called this set up Bretton Woods Mark II, after the postwar system of fixed exchange rates. They see it as a relatively benign and stable arrangement, in which developing economies are able to grow fast by fixing their exchange rates against the currency of the biggest developed economy, and then lend back to the US the dollars they earn in the process, permitting it to continue buying their exports.[87] But the benefits to the US went considerably further. Wolf points out that, at the end of 2006, 'almost two-thirds of the foreign holdings of US assets (other than financial derivatives) took the form of debt'. But the real return on American private and public debt held by foreigners was, over the period 1973 to 2004, a mere 0.32 per cent. 'Thus, the signal – and for the United States, very favourable – characteristic of foreign ownership is that a high proportion of foreign capital is invested in assets with low returns, denominated – even better for the United States – in depreciated dollars.'[88]

If this analysis is correct, then Leo Panitch and Martijn Konings are mistaken when they argue that 'much of this capital came to the US for reasons of prudent investment and profitability'.[89] Indeed, Wolf calculates that America's net financial liabilities – what it owes to foreigners minus its assets abroad (the foreign investments of US firms and citizens) – has risen much more slowly than the influx of capital required to finance the deficit. Simply on the basis of the cumulative current account deficits, 'the US should have had net liabilities equal to 44 percent of GDP at the end of 2006. As it was, according to the Bureau of Economic Analysis, the net liability position was only 16 percent of GDP, down from 23 percent at the end of 2002.'[90] This is partly because of the fall of the dollar against other major currencies (most recently in 2002–8), but mainly because the prices of US-held assets abroad have risen relative to those of the assets held by foreigners in the US.

Wolf concludes that 'the best argument for the view that high current account deficits are indefinitely sustainable is that Americans are "savvy investors", fleecing the naive'. Indeed: 'The United States (as is true also of the United Kingdom) has been a vast and hitherto very profitable hedge fund.' This state of affairs has allowed the US to continue to play a hegemonic role:

> The United States accommodates and offsets whatever the rest of the world throws at it because, as issuer of the world's key currency, it suffers from no external constraint: it has been able, at least up to now, to borrow as much as it wishes in its own currency, at modest interest rates . . . The result is that the Federal Reserve is free to pursue policies that balance the US economy and, in doing so, also balance the world's, by absorbing the excess savings and so the surplus of goods and services, at given real exchange rates, of the rest of the world.[91]

This performance, in which the US used its power to issue dollars, unbacked by gold, to finance a chronic balance of payments deficit, is a bit like the shape that Ludwig Wittgenstein called a duck-rabbit because, depending on the angle from which you looked at it, it resembled a duck or a rabbit.[92] From one angle, it is an index of continued US hegemony; from another, it suggests how precarious this hegemony has now become, resting as it does, not on the outflows of capital through which Britain financed the economic expansion of the late nineteenth century or the US the reconstruction of European and Japanese capitalism after 1945, but on a massive inflow of capital from one of the poorest countries in the world. Nevertheless, for a generation, the Dollar Wall-Street Regime worked, at least for those in whose interests it was constructed. It provided the framework in which globalized financial markets expanded spectacularly. The new pattern of economic expansion in the US itself was set during the recovery from the recession of the early 1980s, spurred by a massive rise in military expenditure, which was initiated under Jimmy Carter and accelerated by Ronald Reagan, and involving widespread restructuring of industrial and commercial capital, a soaring stock market, and a mergers and acquisition craze that pioneered many of the techniques used on a far larger scale during the credit boom of the 2000s – for example, leveraged buyouts financed by massive borrowing that were essentially bets that dismantling the target corporation would, by allowing some assets to be sold off and the rest (and the surviving workforce) to be ruthlessly squeezed, generate enough profits to pay off the loans and reward the organizers of the takeover.[93]

One consequence was much greater financial instability. The stock-market boom came to an abrupt end when Wall Street crashed in October 1987. Another turning point seemed to come in September 1998, when the financial turbulence that followed Russia's defaulting on its foreign debt precipitated the collapse of a leading US hedge fund, Long Term Capital Management (LTCM). But, in another key element in the new pattern, the Fed under Greenspan came to the rescue on both occasions – in the first case promising to provide whatever liquidity was needed to keep the markets afloat, in the second brigading leading Wall Street banks into bailing out LTCM and thereby helping to restore confidence.[94] More severe financial crises resulting in major recessions did happen, but – with the exception of Japan – they didn't affect the advanced economies. The victims were to be found elsewhere, in East and Southeast Asia, Latin America, Turkey and

Russia. Some radical scholars, for example, Panitch and Konings, argue that, not simply has 'liberalized finance proved to be "functional" for both global accumulation and American empire', but that financial crises have also had a beneficial effect, especially for US capitalism, since they 'may be exploited to reduce or remove barriers to capitalist interests that "ordinary" market or diplomatic pressures could not'.[95] The great East Asian crisis was widely seen, not least in the affected countries themselves, as an opportunity seized by Washington, in tandem with the IMF, to lever open economies whose model of capitalism, based on close interconnections between the state, banks and industrial firms, had hitherto made them relatively impenetrable by American capital.[96]

Certainly the processes of financialization contributed significantly to the shift in income from labour to capital. Thus Bryan and Rafferty argue that financial derivatives, by making all forms of capital commensurable, have promoted the intensification of labour in the neoliberal era: 'The process of commensuration of capital on a global scale requires labour in each location to deliver "competitive" rates of wages and productivity to ensure globally competitive rates of return on capital.'[97] The effect of the different ways in which labour was put under relentless pressure, combined with changes in the tax and welfare systems, was, above all in the US and Britain, a substantial redistribution of wealth and income from poor to rich. One striking feature of this redistribution was the tendency of those at the top of the class structure to take an important part of their income, not as a return on ownership assets, but as salary and related benefits deriving from their occupation of senior executive positions. According to Mohun, '[t]he growing extraction of surplus value out of productive labour, which is so marked a feature of the US economy after 1979, was appropriated not as corporate profits, but primarily as the labour incomes of supervisory workers'.[98]

This redistribution helped to give the mid-2000s, after the economic and terrorist scares at the beginning of that decade, the feeling of a new *belle époque*, comparable to

that of a hundred years before.[99] The corporate rich and
the upper middle class enjoyed the benefits of higher
incomes, of real and financial assets whose monetary value
soared yearly, and of what came to be celebrated as, in the
words of Ben Bernanke, Federal Reserve Governor, 'the
Great Moderation' in inflation and economic instability,
as the influx of cheap manufactures from China forced
down the rate at which consumer prices increased.[100]
Financial crises might occur, but Greenspan, the presiding
economic deity of the era, was there, even after Bernanke
had succeeded him as Chairman of the Fed, to offer reas-
surance that such turbulence was an inescapable accompaniment to capitalism's prosperity-spreading dynamism.
After the worst of the East Asian crisis was over, Greenspan, along with US Treasury Secretary Robert Rubin
and his deputy, Lawrence Summers, was pictured smiling
smugly on the front page of *Time* as 'The Committee to
Save the World'. Even radical critics of neoliberalism
seemed to place great faith in the American state's powers
of crisis management. According to Panitch and Konings,
'the fact that financial crises are now such a common event
is only half the story . . . The other half of the story . . . is
that over this same period [the 1980s and 1990s], the
capacity to cope with these crises has also grown.'[101] A
decade after the East Asian crisis, Greenspan and Rubin
were disgraced figures – the former because of his responsibility for the housing bubble, the latter for his role at
Citigroup, which was driven close to bankruptcy during
the financial crisis – and Summers was Barack Obama's
chief economic adviser, helping the new President grapple
with the worst economic slump since the 1930s. What had
gone wrong?

Economic growth increasingly driven by financial bubbles

The year 1997 emerges in retrospect as a turning point for
the world economy. This is partly because of the severe

economic and financial crisis that afflicted East Asia, which was already increasingly seen as the dynamo of global capitalism. But it was also because it marked the historical moment at which, as we have seen, the recovery in US profitability peaked, and thereafter went into partial reverse. The pressure on American industrial and commercial firms was reinforced by the rise of the dollar against other currencies from 1995 onwards, which undermined their competitiveness relative to foreign rivals. Given the weight that the US continued to exert within the world economy (see Table 1.3), these depressive forces represented an important constraint on future expansion. Those managing American capitalism in particular had to try to keep the economy growing on the basis of a weaker foundation than during the period, from the early 1980s to the late 1990s, when the rate of profit was rising.

In this context, it is important to understand that the installation of the neoliberal economic policy regime did *not* involve the abandonment of macroeconomic management by states. It was therefore not a simple return to classical liberalism. But the objectives, tools, and main locus of macroeconomic management all changed. The objective was now, not to achieve full employment, but to minimize the rate of inflation. The tool was monetary policy, which depended on control of interest rates and of the creation of credit money. New Labour under Tony Blair and Gordon Brown were emblematic of this shift in renouncing an active fiscal policy – 'tax and spend', as they disparagingly referred to it. Finally, the key agents of this policy were central banks, which, if they didn't already have the power to set interest rates, were given that power during the neoliberal era. This institutional shift, and the associated tendency for governments to set inflation targets for central banks, was in part a consequence of the failure, during the 'heroic' era of monetarism in the 1980s, of mechanistic attempts to control the money supply. But in another respect what Edward Luttwak called 'central bankism' deeply accorded with neoliberal ideology, and in

particular with the idea that allowing politicians account-
able to mass electorates to manage the economy would
inevitably lead to inflationary and unsustainable policies.
The solution proved to lie in relying on the discretion of
central bankers, institutionally insulated from the normal
pressures of capitalist democracy, to use the techniques at
their command to keep inflation low and the economy on
the right track.[102]

This explains the prominence that figures such as
Volcker and Greenspan came to occupy during the neoliberal era. But the latter's task became increasingly difficult
as the second millennium drew to a close (particularly
since the Fed, unlike other central banks, has a statutory
duty to maintain long-term growth, as well as low inflation). Greenspan reacted to the LTCM crisis, not merely
by mounting a rescue, but with a series of interest-rate
cuts, feeding the growing speculative bubble that had
already been expanding in the stock market, particularly
around IT-related shares. This stimulated demand for
goods and services thanks to the 'wealth effect': upper-
middle-class households borrowed and spent more on the
strength of the higher monetary value of the securities they
owned. Brenner writes:

> In order to keep the US and the world economy from
> serious trouble, the Fed thus had little choice but to depend
> upon the continued ascent of the stock market to maintain
> the accelerated growth of US domestic consumption and
> investment. In effect, the Fed was sustaining a new form
> of artificial demand and stimulus by means of increased
> *private* debt, both corporate and consumer, made possible
> by the rise of equity prices and the resulting wealth effect,
> rather than relying on the old Keynesian formula based on
> public deficits.[103]

This essay in 'stock-market Keynesianism' did lead to
genuinely productive investment – or, more accurately,
overinvestment: during the late 1990s the booming
telecommunications industry laid 39 million miles of

fibre-optic line in the US, enough to circle the globe 1566 times.[104] But productive capital was been driven by a stock-market bubble, most evident in the frenzy (on both sides of the Atlantic) for the shares of Internet firms most of which made no profits. The dotcom bubble burst in the spring of 2000, helping to precipitate a potentially severe recession that was dominated by massive industrial over-capacity and corporate debt. Greenspan, responding to the double shock of the economic downturn and 9/11, cut interest rates to the bone, till by June 2003 they hit 1 per cent. He explained: 'We wanted to shut down the possibil-ity of corrosive deflation; we were willing to chance that by cutting rates we might foster a bubble, an inflationary boom of some sort, which we would subsequently have to address.'[105] This strategy worked in the short term: in effect, the bubble migrated from the stock market to housing. As Brenner put it in a prescient article published in 2004:

> Once more Greenspan has thus sought to push up asset prices, inflating paper wealth, in order to enhance the capacity to borrow and thereby to spend. But, in the wake of the deep fall of profitability from 1997 and of equity prices from the middle of 2000, as well as corporations' preoccupation with reducing indebtedness by cutting back on borrowing, he has had to shift emphasis. The Fed is still attempting to boost the stock market to improve the finan-cial condition of corporations and the business outlook more generally. But it has had to place its hopes for stimu-lating the economy primarily on driving down mortgage rates and pushing up housing prices, so as to pave the way for increased household borrowing and consumer spend-ing (including investment in houses). In their own terms, these hopes have been spectacularly realized.[106]

House prices in the US rose by 56 per cent in the five years to the peak of the market in the third quarter of 2005.[107] The housing bubble was an international phenomenon, affecting a number of other economies – among them,

Britain, Spain, southern Ireland and Singapore. Once again the wealth effect kicked in: households, encouraged by the rise in property values and rock-bottom lending costs, increased borrowing and spending. In 2005, US households extracted $750bn against the monetary value of their homes, two-thirds of which was spent on personal consumption, home improvements and credit-card debt.[108] The resulting surge in personal consumption (along with a sharp increase in public expenditure fuelled by the war on terrorism and a rise in American competitiveness thanks to the fall in the dollar promoted by the Bush administration) pulled the US out of recession and helped to put the entire world economy on a boom path. This was the historical moment of Bretton Woods Mark II. The flow of capital and commodities across the Pacific from China to the US fed the expansion of both economies and drew others in, with Germany, Japan and South Korea supplying complex industrial goods and components for Chinese assembly plants and primary producers in Africa and Latin America feeding their apparently limitless appetite for raw materials.

It was this apparently virtuous circle that led the IMF as late as the autumn of 2007, after the collapse of the housing boom and the onset of the credit crunch, to celebrate global capitalism's breakthrough into a new golden era:

> From 2004 to the present, the world economy has enjoyed its strongest period of sustained growth since the late 1960s and early 1970s, while inflation has remained at low levels. Not only has recent global growth been high but the expansion has also been broadly shared across countries. The volatility of growth has fallen, which may seem especially surprising because the more volatile emerging market and developing countries account for a rising share of the global economy.[109]

This remarkably hubristic document went on to run dangerously close to predicting the disappearance of the business cycle: 'A comparison of business cycles over the past century points to a secular increase in the length of expansions and a decrease in the amount of time economies spend in recessions. In advanced economies, deep recessions have virtually disappeared in the post–World War II period.' The economic crises of the mid- and late-1970s were dismissed as 'a temporary break from the trend of ever-longer expansions in moderately growing advanced economies'.[110] Accompanying such complacency about the 'Great Moderation' was euphoria about the BRICs – the leading emerging market economies of Brazil, Russia, India and China – whose ascent was widely seen as promising a secure future for global capitalism. The acronym was invented by Goldman Sachs; the idea helped to keep the great bubble of financial speculation expanding. Indeed, as Graham Turner has demonstrated, the boom of the mid-2000s involved a global credit bubble, as speculative capital poured into favoured economies in the South and in central and eastern Europe.[111]

Three features made this latest bubble particularly dangerous. The first was its dependence on the US–China circuit. It was, as we have seen, the flow of capital from East Asia that kept interest rates low and hence made the boom in personal consumption possible. But this symbiosis of two economies – one geared to high consumption, the other to high investment, both seen (by themselves as well as by others) as potential, if not actual, geopolitical rivals – seemed like a tenuous basis for a sustained path of global capital accumulation. At the height of the boom, household consumption amounted to 67 per cent of GDP in the US, but only 33 per cent in China.[112] An increasing volume of elite policy debate focused on the dangers posed by 'global imbalances' and the need to address them. Bernanke made an influential speech in March 2005 arguing that the US deficit was a consequence of a 'global savings glut' centred in East Asia.[113] Nothing of any significance was done in practice, no doubt because the existing setup was so favourable to the two key players in Washington and Beijing.

Secondly, the credit bubble of the mid-2000s marked the apogee of the new system of Anglo-American speculative finance. The shadow banking system that we discussed earlier in this chapter engaged in a frenzy of the kind of innovation that Minsky argues plays a key role in destabilizing financial markets. The drive was to take advantage of the cheap credit conditions to build up leverage as high as possible and thereby to maximize profits. Credit derivatives – above all, collateralized debt obligations – and the structured investment vehicles that acted as conduits for their sale played a key role getting lending off banks' balance sheets by selling the loans on in as high a volume as possible. The global market for derivatives rose from $41 trillion to $677 trillion in 1997–2007.[114] Loans to less safe debtors – for example, subprime mortgages – were particularly attractive, because the higher the risk, the higher the interest and fees that would be charged. And the credit ratings agencies, eager to keep in with the banks that were paying their fees, were on hand to certify many CDOs as triple-AAA investments, almost safe from default.

The easy availability of cheap credit encouraged financial institutions to repeat the pattern of earlier bubbles, borrowing short to lend long – a practice that made them highly vulnerable when credit dried up. As Adair Turner put it,

> a wide range of institutions – both banks and near banks – developed an increasing reliance on 'liquidity through marketability', believing it safe to hold long term to maturity assets funded by short-term liabilities on the grounds that the assets could be sold rapidly in liquid markets if needed. This assumption was valid at the level of firms individually in non-crisis conditions, but became rapidly invalid in mid 2007, as many firms attempted simultaneous liquidation of positions.[115]

This proliferating web of speculation depended on close relationships between financial firms and complaisant public authorities. An investigation conducted after the crash by the Center for Public Integrity revealed that the top 25 US originators of subprime mortgages – responsible between them for $1,000bn in subprime mortgages in 2005–7, almost three-quarters of the total, had spent almost $370m since the late 1990s in Washington on lobbying and campaign donations to prevent tighter regulation of their activities. Roland Arnall, founder and chief executive of Ameriquest Mortgage Co, which issued $80bn of subprime mortgages in 2005–7, was appointed US Ambassador to the Netherlands by the Bush administration. Twenty-one of these companies, most of which were bankrupted by the subprime crisis, were either owned or heavily financed by big banks such as Citigroup, Goldman Sachs, Wells Fargo, JPMorgan and Bank of America – all of which benefited heavily from the subsequent government bailout.[116]

The most important actors in (and beneficiaries from) this process were thus the major American banks, now finally liberated from the confines of Glass–Steagall: according to one study, US banks' unprecedented profitability in the decade before the onset of the crisis reflected how the high level of concentration in the sector permitted the extraction of monopoly rents from the rest of the economy.[117] But London (not just the historical City, but its eastern and western offshoots in, respectively, Canary Wharf and Mayfair) became in many ways the most important venue for the credit bubble. London accounted for nearly half of global credit derivatives turnover in 1998 and over a third of the much bigger market in 2006. London's rise to challenge, and by some measures overtake New York as the world's biggest financial centre in part reflected the growing importance of Europe in global finance. By 2007 Europe accounted for over a third of global investment banking revenues, with over half the turnover passing through London.[118] Gillian Tett suggests that London's pivotal role in the shadow banking system was also a consequence of the way in which European firms responded to the launch of the euro in 1999 by moving away from their traditional reliance on bank loans 'straight to using derivatives, rather than cash-based instruments such as bonds. It was a "leapfrogging" pattern, comparable to what happens when developing nations discover telephones and move straight to using mobile phones rather than messing around with landlines.'[119]

Hedge funds and private equity firms were also attracted to set up shop in London by the extremely hospitable policies pursued by New Labour after its election in May 1997. In his second budget, Gordon Brown cut capital gains tax to 10 per cent, a move that proved particularly favourable to hedge funds and private equity firms. When the US Congress responded to the scandals and scams of the dotcom boom – Enron, WorldCom and the like – by tightening up financial regulation with the Sarbanes–Oxley Act, Britain boasted of its 'light-touch' regime. Philip Augar describes the Financial Services and Markets Act 2001 as 'more like a mandate to protect the UK's financial services industry than to regulate it. The regulator was "not to discourage the launch of new financial products" and had to avoid "erecting regulatory barriers" . . . [and] ". . . consider the international mobility of financial businesses"'. Brown's final speech as Chancellor of the Exchequer at the City's annual Mansion House Dinner in June 2007 celebrated 'London's position . . . not only as the international financial centre of the world but of global pre-eminence' and congratulated himself for avoiding 'a regulatory crackdown' after the financial bust at the beginning of the decade.[120]

One reason why such remarks so strongly invited nemesis was that, thirdly, the credit boom rested on notably weak foundations in the productive economy. The Keynesian economist Wynne Godley has, since the late 1990s, acted as a lonely Cassandra, documenting the extent to which the continued expansion on the US economy has become dependent on the continual growth of private sector debt, reflecting an ultimately unsustainable decline in saving by both firms and households.[121] This 'permanent debt economy', as Chris Harman describes it, was a pronounced feature of the credit boom: in 2007 personal debt reached 139 per cent of disposable income in the US and 173.1 per cent in Britain, the highest in the advanced economies.[122] This pattern – and its counterpart, high saving levels in China and elsewhere in East Asia – requires closer analysis. Concepts such as savings and investment used in analysis of global imbalances refer to macroeconomic aggregates whose understanding Keynes helped to pioneer. Despite their undoubted usefulness, these concepts grasp the behaviour of capitalist economies at a relatively superficial level. To go deeper, we need the Marxist concept of capitalist relations of production and the understanding of antagonistic class relationships that this allows. Patterns of consumption reflect deeply entrenched class relations. These realities are occasionally registered in Martin Wolf's analysis of global imbalances:

> Chinese households save enormously. But the core of the Chinese savings story over the past five or six years has been the rise in corporate savings . . . The Chinese government told state enterprises to become profitable, and they have done what they were told. The corporate sector has become profitable by disposing of surplus workers, yet the government has not taken some of the increased profits as dividends on the assets it owns, even to finance a safety net for displaced workers. Remarkably (and shockingly), the government has left the money with enterprise insiders. But the government itself is also a large saver. China has about 800 million poor people, yet the country now consumes less than half of GDP and exports capital to the rest of the world. This is highly peculiar. It is also why the country has such a huge current account surplus.[123]

So what is generally presented as 'China' not consuming 'enough' is really, from the perspective of Marxist value theory, intensified exploitation via the extraction of relative surplus-value – fewer workers are producing a growing output. Low consumption by Chinese workers is matched

by high profits for Chinese capital. But the same realities
govern the other end of the circuit that has sustained the
world economy, namely the US. Analysing the American
balance of payments deficit, Wolf points to

> a startling contrast between business and the household
> sector . . . The business sector moved into a large deficit
> during the investment boom triggered by the bubble
> economy of the late 1990s and 2000. It then cut back
> sharply on investment and, after a short period of squeeze,
> built up profits again. More important, it also avoided any
> repeat of the investment surge of the 1990s. As a result,
> the business sector ran a financial surplus from the fourth
> quarter of 2001 to the first quarter of 2007.[124]

So the gap between savings and investment is to be found
in the US business sector; I'll return to this shortly. Let's
first note that, as Wolf observes, '[t]he household sector is
quite a different story. It has been running historically
unprecedented financial deficits, consistently spending
more than its income on consumption and residential
investment.'[125] The obvious way of interpreting this is
that ordinary Americans have been engaged in a high-
consumption splurge. Such a view informs all the chatter
about the crisis being 'our' fault because we've been so
busy borrowing and spending. The trouble is that this
doesn't fit with another important piece of the economic
puzzle. As Edward Luce puts it,

> [b]etween 2000 and 2006, the US economy expanded by
> 18 per cent, whereas real income for the median working
> household dropped by 1.1 per cent in real terms, or about
> $2,000 . . . Meanwhile, the top tenth saw an improvement
> of 32 per cent in their incomes, the top 1 per cent a rise
> of 203 per cent and the top 0.1 per cent a gain of 425 per
> cent.
>
> Part of this was because the latest period of economic
> growth failed to create jobs at nearly the same rate as in
> previous business cycles and even led to a decline in the

number of hours worked for most employees. Unusually
for a time of expansion, the number of participants in the
labour force also fell. But mostly it was because the fruits
of economic growth and soaring productivity rates went
to the highest income earners.[126]

One hasn't to look much further than these figures to
understand the deep anger in American society that has
been directed against the Wall Street bankers. But they also
represent, once again, a higher rate of exploitation thanks
to an increase in relative surplus-value. Workers at both
ends of the circuit have been squeezed. The difference is
that Chinese workers, at a much lower standard of living
than their counterparts in the US, are pressured to save in
order to provide the security against illness, unemployment and old age that the Chinese state no longer offers
them. American workers, by contrast, have been encouraged to borrow in order to sustain their basic consumption
at a time when their real wages have actually fallen. This
both helped to maintain effective demand and thereby to
keep the American and world economies growing after the
collapse of the dotcom boom in 2000 and to provide
profits for the banks that lent them the money. It is the
bursting of the resulting bubble that precipitated the
present crisis.[127]

But there is one final piece to the puzzle. As we have
seen, Wolf argues that American firms were hanging onto
their profits rather than investing them. But he also noted
that this is a general phenomenon since

> what we may now confidently call the global stock market
> bubble of 1999–2000. In most economically significant
> countries, corporations are very profitable but cautious
> about investing . . . The shift on income from labour to
> capital is an important phenomenon across high-income
> economies. Interestingly and significantly, the biggest
> shift from labour income has not been in the United States
> and other Anglo-Saxon countries, but in Japan and the
> euro-zone.[128]

So one key dimension of the 'savings glut' is that capitalists in the advanced economies during the 2000s increased their profits through wage repression but then did not invest these profits in expanded production. Hence the gap between savings and investment stressed by Bernanke and Wolf shouldn't be understood primarily as deriving from differences between regions of the world economy, but in terms of the antagonistic class interests that cut across regions and nations. The evidence available suggests that capitalists may have succeeded in increasing the rate of surplus-value, the mass of profits relative to wages, but they have failed to push up the rate of *profit*, the mass of profits relative to total investment (in means of production as well as in labour-power), to a level where they feel confident enough to invest on a large scale. If this explanation is correct, then we can definitely see the credit bubble as an effort to allow the US economy (and hence, thanks to its central role in maintaining global demand, the world) to continue to grow, despite its failure to overcome a chronic crisis of profitability and overaccumulation that dates ultimately back to the 1960s.

In the light of these underlying weaknesses, the global economic and financial crisis was an accident waiting to happen.[129] The precipitant was provided first by a series of interest rate increases that the Fed began in June 2004, hoping to calm the economy down gently. The effect was to squeeze subprime borrowers and, from the spring of 2006, to start a slide in house prices. Initially, however, the housing slowdown was accompanied by an acceleration of the markets in CDOs and CDSs, as banks increased their leverage in a feverish hunt after diminishing profit margins (though a few, notably Deutsche Bank and Goldman Sachs, started to bet on a housing bust). It was symbolic that, amid this fever, Northern Rock, hitherto an obscure bank in the northeast of England and soon to be the first great victim of the crisis, was given an award in January 2007 for 'best financial borrower' in recognition of its success in financing half its £68bn mortgage book with mortgage-backed bonds held all over the world.[130] The continuing demand for cheap debt was driven also by the private equity firms responsible for a wave of highly leveraged takeovers. The competitive pressure on even the largest banks to continue feeding the bubble with more lending was summed up by Chuck Prince, chief executive officer of Citigroup, in July 2007, on the very eve of the financial crisis that would, within months, sweep him from office: 'as long as the music is playing, you've got to get up and dance. We're still dancing.'[131] By 2007 the Wall Street banks' leverage ratios (loans to equity) had soared to record levels – x25 at Goldman Sachs, x29 at Lehman Brothers, x32 at Merrill Lynch, x33 at Bear Stearns and Morgan Stanley.[132]

As mortgage defaults increased sharply in 2006–7, the entire speculative house of cards erected by the banks and their partners in the shadow banking system began to fall apart. Or, to change metaphors, the financial system proved to be like a piece of knitting that pulling on a loose strand of wool threatens to unravel entirely. The crisis in the subprime sector undermined the market for mortgage-backed securities, and thereby hauled down the prices of the CDOs into which these securities had been bundled. But, since CDOs – and the credit default swaps (CDSs) used to insure against default – had been taken up throughout the entire financial system, in Europe as well as the US, the entire system seized up. This became visible with the onset of the credit crunch proper. It began on 9 August 2007, when BNP Paribas froze access to one of its major money market funds and the European Central Bank reacted by pumping what proved to be €94bn into the financial markets, prompting the Fed to follow suit. But banks, worried about their own losses and suspicious of others' plight, stopped lending to each other.

The more vulnerable institutions – those that had particularly overextended themselves – began to collapse: the most notable initial victims were Northern Rock, eventually nationalized, and Bear Stearns, taken over by

JPMorgan Chase, after catastrophic collapses in confidence. The efforts of the Fed and other central banks aggressively to counteract the credit crunch by pumping liquidity into the financial system and cutting interest rates presumed that the main problem was that banks were short of money because the wholesale markets had frozen up. But, increasingly it became clear, especially after the Bush administration allowed Lehman Brothers to go bust in September 2008, that the problem was one of solvency: the losses of a number of major banks threatened to destroy them, and with them the entire financial system. And so the autumn and winter of 2008–9 saw an astonishing toppling of financial giants – Merrill Lynch taken over by Bank of America, Fannie Mae, Freddie Mac, AIG, Royal Bank of Scotland and Lloyds Banking Group (itself having absorbed Halifax Bank of Scotland) all placed under the effective control of their governments, Goldman Sachs and Morgan Stanley, the last of the five Wall Street investment banks left standing, taking refuge in holding company status.

Meanwhile, the financial crisis morphed into a general economic slump. Initially much faith was placed in the idea – a hangover from the credit boom – that, even if the immediately affected economies, notably the US and Britain, might suffer recessions, China and the rest of Asia could somehow 'decouple' from America and keep the world economy growing despite the financial crisis.[133] This proved to be the merest fantasy: the American recession that started at the end of 2007 now sent the great manufacturing and trading economies of the world – Germany, Japan, China – into a tailspin as the biggest export market dried up. The OECD predicted that Japan would shrink by 6.6 per cent in 2009 and Germany by 5.3 per cent, while the US would contract by a 'mere' 4 per cent and Britain by 3.7 per cent. A key mechanism at work in generating the very pronounced global economic contraction in late 2008 and early 2009 was the descent of international trade into 'free fall', as the OECD put it. World real trade growth, after averaging 7 per cent a year in

1996–2005, and peaking at 9.5 per cent in 2006, dropped to 2.5 per cent in 2008 and a projected minus 13.2 per cent in 2009.[134] Even China's stormy growth rate collapsed, according to estimates by Goldman Sachs and JPMorgan, to 2.2 per cent in the last quarter of 2008, rising to 5.8 per cent in the following quarter, still sluggish by Beijing's standards.[135] The 'Great Moderation' had abruptly come to an end, not with a whimper, but with an almighty bang.

Dilemmas of recovery

One notable advantage enjoyed by policy-makers confronted with the global economic and financial crisis in comparison to their predecessors in the 1930s lay in the much greater economic weight of the state. Minsky estimates: 'A government whose spending is at least 16 per cent and perhaps as high as 20 per cent of prosperity GNP is necessary to protect the economy against a catastrophic decline in investment and profits.'[136] By this criterion, even the more *laissez faire* Anglo-Saxon economies were well-equipped to cope with a severe crisis, with percentage shares of national income taken by state expenditure varying between the low thirties and the mid-forties, while in continental Europe the typical share was somewhere between 45 and 50 per cent (see Table 1.4). Moreover, states did not simply rely on the so-called 'automatic stabilizers' to counteract the fall in effective demand: during recessions government borrowing tends to rise, maintaining effective demand, as tax revenues fall and public expenditure rises, thanks to the increase in bankruptcies and unemployment. Additional fiscal stimulus packages were introduced further increasing public spending and cutting taxes: in the OECD area these packages averaged about 2.5 per cent of national income in 2008–10, though the Obama administration's amounted to a thumping 5.6 per cent of 2008 GDP.[137]

Table 1.4 Government expenditure as a share of GDP, 2005

Country	% GDP
Australia	32.9
Austria	45.0
Belgium	47.3
Canada	39.5
Denmark	51.2
Finland	45.8
France	49.8
Germany	46.2
Ireland, Republic of	37.5
Italy	46.4
Japan	30.9
Netherlands	45.7
Norway	42.8
New Zealand	34.7
Sweden	52.0
Switzerland	36.4
UK	44.7
US	36.6

Source: C. Hay, 'Globalization's Impact on States', in J. Ravenhill, ed., *Global Political Economy* (Oxford, 2007), Table 10.1, p. 327

The money that states threw at the economy is one major reason why the 'Great Recession' (as many came to call the slump) is unlikely to be as severe as the Great Depression of the 1930s. But it does not follow that the world economy will rapidly resume a path of rapid growth. In April 2009 a chastened IMF published a re-examination of the patterns of boom and slump that had only eighteen months earlier led it to celebrate a new Golden Age of capitalism. It was alarmed by two of its findings. First, 'recessions associated with financial crises have been more severe and longer lasting than recessions associated with other shocks. Recoveries from such recessions have been typically slower, associated with weak domestic demand

and tight credit conditions.' Secondly, 'recessions that are highly synchronized across countries have been longer and deeper than those confined to one region. Recoveries from these recessions have typically been weak', because it's much harder to recover by increasing exports if the entire world economy is depressed. The IMF concluded: 'The implications of these findings for the current situation are sobering. The current downturn is highly synchronized and is associated with a deep financial crisis, a rare combination in the postwar period. Accordingly, the downturn is likely to be unusually severe, and the recovery is expected to be sluggish.'[138]

More than anything else, as the IMF acknowledged, it is this pattern – a generalized economic crisis interwoven with a major financial crash – that invites comparison with the Great Depression. Then also a developing economic recession reflecting a fall in the rate of profit interacted with the bursting of a financial bubble – the Wall Street crash of October 1929 – to generate the collapse of the banking system and a global slump.[139] But why should this combination be so devastating economically? Richard Koo, Chief Economist of the Nomura Research Institute, has written an intriguing comparison of the Great Depression with the long Japanese economic crisis of the 1990s and early 2000s. Koo argues that both were cases of what he calls a balance-sheet recession. The dominant feature of such recessions is that a collapse in asset prices has left a large number of firms technically insolvent. In other words, their liabilities – the loans they took out to buy assets or on the strength of their ownership of these assets – are greater than their assets. Where these firms are able to avoid bankruptcy, they cut investment to a minimum and concentrate on paying off their debts. Unless counteracted, the effect is a substantial fall in effective demand, driving the economy into recession. 'Monetary policy is impotent during a balance-sheet recession', Koo argues. The kind of measures taken by the Bank of Japan in the 1990s and by the Fed and the Bank of England in response

to the present crisis – to stimulate demand by cutting interest rates to zero or close to zero and buying up government
and high-quality corporate bonds as a way of pumping
money into the financial system (quantitative easing) –
presume that the problem is a matter of an inadequate
supply of money. But a balance-sheet recession involves a
fall in the *demand* for money:

> after the bubble collapsed in Japan, not only were there no
> willing borrowers, but existing borrowers were paying
> down debt – and they were doing so when interest rates
> were at zero. Technically insolvent companies, struggling
> to pay down debt and repair balance sheets hit by the
> nationwide plunge in asset prices, were not interested in
> borrowing, regardless of how far the central bank lowered
> rates.[140]

A balance-sheet recession is a collective action problem
(what Koo calls a 'fallacy of composition'): what it is
individually rational for firms to do – pay off their debts
– has a collectively sub-optimal outcome, economic contraction. Until firms have got their balance-sheets back
into the black and become net investors again, the only
effective force capable of countering the decline in effective
demand is fiscal policy – government borrowing and
spending:

> if the government simply stands by and watches, the
> economy will fall into the kind of catastrophic deflationary
> spiral seen in the US between 1929 and 1933. To stop this
> vicious circle, the government has only one option: it must
> do precisely the opposite of what the private sector is
> doing. In other words it must borrow (and spend) the
> savings that the private sector can no longer use.[141]

This analysis has considerable implications for the present
crisis. Deleveraging – in other words, financial institutions
and households seeking to reduce their debts – has been a
critical factor driving the world economy into slump.

Faced with huge losses, banks reduce lending. Firms, denied credit, slash output, lay off workers, and cut wages. Households, to deal with the disappearance of easy credit and the threat of unemployment, start or increase saving, which reduces effective demand. The knock-on effects – lower sales, redundancies, bankruptcies – can then feed back into the financial system, as banks, faced with greater losses, further cut back on lending, generating further rounds of feedback via the impact of these decisions on households and firms. In 2008–9 cross-border lending fell faster than the general decline in credit. Emerging market economies, which had benefited from an influx of speculative capital during the credit boom (net private inflows peaked at 5 per cent of emerging market GDP in 2007), were particularly hard hit. The IMF estimates that many central and east European economies, which had blown up huge speculative bubbles after their entry into the European Union in 2004, would suffer an outflow of bank loans equivalent to 5 per cent of GDP – comparable to the reversal of capital flows that devastated Latin America in the early 1980s and East and Southeast Asia in the late 1990s.[142]

More seriously still for the system, banks and other financial institutions continue to struggle with huge losses. In April 2009 the IMF raised its estimate of the total bad loans that would to be written off in 2007–10 to $4.1 trillion – $2.7 trillion originating in the US, the rest in Europe and Japan. It also calculated that the capital injections necessary to get banks' ratio of assets to total common equity back to pre-crisis levels (×25) would cost $275bn in the US, about $375bn in the euro-zone, about $125 billion in the UK, and about $100bn in the rest of 'mature Europe' (Switzerland and Scandinavia). Returning leverage to the levels of the mid-1990s (×17), would cost $500 billion in the US, about $725bn in the euro-zone, about $250bn in the UK, and about $225bn in the rest of 'mature Europe'. Only the state could possibly come up with such huge injections of capital, which require further increases

in government borrowing. These would come in addition
to the bank bailouts in 2008–9, which the IMF estimated
cost 12.7 per cent of GDP in the US and 9.1 per cent in
Britain.[143]

Moreover, the effective insolvency of the banking
system, like the economic crisis, is not just an Anglo-
American problem. In the spring of 2009 the *Süddeutsche
Zeitung* published an internal memo from BaFin, the
German banking regulator, estimating that the scale of the
bank write-offs would be more than €800bn, about a third
of Germany's annual GDP, compared to the capital and
reserves of its monetary and financial institutions amount-
ing to only €441.5bn.[144]

It's hardly surprising that, in the light of such mind-
boggling and frightening numbers, a major ideological and
political polarization developed within and between the
leading capitalist states, as we saw in the Introduction.
Roughly speaking the division is between the proponents
of fiscal expansion and of fiscal consolidation. The first –
represented, for example, at the G20 summit in April 2009
by the US and Japanese governments – argued that the
priority lay in expanding government borrowing and
spending to counteract the contractionary forces at work.
Their opponents – notably the German and French governments – warned against the economically damaging consequences of the growing public sector debt and therefore
resisted pressure from the Obama administration for a
large and internationally coordinated fiscal stimulus. A
similar polarization also existed within states – in Britain,
for example, having initially responded to the financial
crash by ostentatiously donning Keynesian garb, the New
Labour government was forced, thanks to its domestic
weakness, to retreat in response to a campaign over the
rapid increase in government debt waged by both the Conservative opposition and Mervyn King, the Governor of the
Bank of England, from supporting Obama's stimulus call.

The same polarization was also at work during the
Great Depression. Although Franklin Roosevelt's New

Deal is conventionally associated with Keynesian economics, his administration was in fact a venue for intense and ideologically charged struggles over economic policy. The initial conflict involved Roosevelt resisting pressure from the wing of the Democratic Party, associated with Wall Street, that wanted to continue the strategy pursued by preceding Republican administrations and symbolized by his immediate predecessor, Herbert Hoover, of, internationally, a close financial and geopolitical alignment with Britain and, domestically, maintaining economic liberal orthodoxy and balanced budgets. Crucially, bracketing his prior ideological commitment to the liberal internationalism of Woodrow Wilson, Roosevelt sabotaged the World Economic and Monetary Conference held in London in June 1933 and embraced a policy of devaluing the dollar by buying gold as a way of halting the deflationary spiral. This crucial shift created the space within which the American state could develop measures capable reviving the economy. In reality, a variety of at least partially inconsistent options were canvassed and to some degree pursued; these ranged from the cartellization of industries and public works programmes mandated by the National Industrial Recovery Act 1933 (which was eventually struck down by the Supreme Court) to various proposals for large-scale planning in some cases based on 'stagnationist' theories that affirmed that mature capitalist economies tended, either because of a shortage of effective demand or of monopolistic corporate structures, towards a less than full employment equilibrium. All these statist programmes were continually resisted by conservative Democrats and Republicans in Congress who demanded a return to balanced budgets.[145]

Balancing between these different forces, Roosevelt steered towards fiscal consolidation after his re-election in 1936, cutting the budget deficit from $4.6bn in fiscal 1936 to $1.4bn in fiscal 1938. The vigorous economic recovery that had set in during the second half of 1936 was cut short: in August and September 1937 recession set in with, as John Strachey puts it, 'a catastrophic swiftness not only as great as, but much greater than, the 1929 slump'. Writing at the time, he puts this down to the victory 'of a general counter-attack against New Deal finance' driven by a school of thought within the administration 'representing the interests and desires of finance capital' that had forced through 'this decisive slashing of the net contribution' by the government to effective demand.[146] Other factors were involved as well in precipitating the 1937–8 recession, for example, a reversal of the build-up of inventories in finished goods in industries such as textiles and steel that drove the previous expansion. Nevertheless, the episode underlines the fragility of an economy recovering from a deep slump such as occurred in the 1930s and as is unfolding today. Koo argues that the 1937–8 recession shows that 'the economy was still in a balance sheet recession and was being kept afloat by fiscal stimulus'. He points to the damaging effects of similar attempts at what he calls 'premature fiscal consolidation' by successive Japanese governments in 1997 and 2001.[147]

The current differences among supporters of fiscal expansion and of fiscal consolidation shouldn't be overstated. On paper at least the German government was projected to be injecting 3.0 per cent of GDP in 2008–10 compared to supposedly Keynesian Britain's more modest 1.4 per cent. Moreover, the stimuli were intended as short-term measures: those governments, such as the US and Britain, that were being forced into much heavier borrowing sought to reassure the financial markets by promising substantial future cuts aimed at moving their budgets closer to balance, once the worst of the economic crisis was over. But, as ever, the kinds of economic policies open to states depended significantly on their relative power within the global capitalist system. Some of the smaller European economies that had experienced the most extreme bubbles during the credit booms were forced into severe austerity programmes at the behest of the European Commission and the IMF. Iceland, for example, was pro-

jected to *cut* spending and raise taxes by the equivalent of
9.4 per cent of GDP in 2008–10 and southern Ireland by
4.4 per cent. The additional funds allocated to the IMF by
the G20 summit in April 2009 would no doubt be used as
a carrot offered to bankrupt states in central and eastern
Europe and elsewhere that would also be required, as a
condition of receiving loans, to implement similar austerity
measures.[148] At the beginning of June 2009 Latvia's central
bank forecast an 18 per cent fall in national income that
year. Having fed the Baltic bubble economies with $75bn
in loans, the Swedish banks were now threatened with
collateral damage, though it would be the populations of
these states, strafed by their rulers' fanatical embrace of
liberal capitalism, who would suffer far more.[149]

But the debate over fiscal policy is a symptom of a
deeper dilemma. As I have tried to show, the present economic and financial crisis is the outcome of a much more
profound and long-term crisis of overaccumulation and
profitability. This latter crisis has various manifestations.
Bernanke's and Woolf's 'savings glut' is one of them, but
so too are the banks' losses – according to the most recent
estimate (October 2009), totalling $3.4 trillion. The routes
to overcoming this long-term crisis involve increasing the
rate of exploitation of labour and a massive devaluation
of capital. Following the first route has not succeeded in
restoring the rate of profit to its levels of the 1950s and
1960s. But the bank rescues represent a powerful obstacle
blocking the second route. The banks' losses represent a
vast amount of unprofitable capital. The bailouts involve
a variety of different measures – injections of capital to
rebuild banks' equity, the purchase of 'troubled' or 'legacy'
assets (mainly the derivatives rendered worthless by the
financial crash), possibly the creation of 'good' and 'bad'
banks, the latter holding these assets with a view to being
sold off once the losses have been finally written off. The
Obama administration also bought up nearly $1½ trillion
of mortgage-backed securities in a determined effort to
drive down mortgage rates and thereby to help reverse the

continuing fall in house prices. Many commentators believe that it will eventually be forced into a much more extensive nationalization of the banks before they can be properly reorganized and recapitalized.

Whatever their precise form, the net effect of these measures will be to keep in existence, albeit restructured and merged, the bulk of the major banks. A major opportunity to destroy a large amount of unprofitable capital will have been thrown away. The same is true of the Washington-induced restructuring of the US auto industry. GM and Chrysler, though bankrupt, will survive, albeit shrunk, perhaps merged with other companies, and largely owned by the US and Canadian governments and union health-care funds. If these rescues work, some of the chronic overcapacity in the world car industry will have been reduced, and the slimmed-down surviving plants will be more competitive, thanks to the concessions made by the United Auto Workers. The fact that the unions will end up as part-owners of firms reorganized at the expense of their members is a stark illustration of the objectivity of the capital-relation that Marx highlighted. But, once again, a major clearout of unprofitable capital will have been avoided. According to an estimate by PwC, the global car industry would produce 86 million vehicles in 2009, but sell only 55 million.[150]

Critics of the bank bailouts frequently register symptoms of the problem. For example, Nassim Nicholas Taleb complains of 'socialisation of losses and privatisation of gains . . . We have managed to combine the worst of capitalism and socialism. In France in the 1980s, the socialists took over the banks. In the US in the 2000s, the banks took over the government. This is surreal.'[151] Indeed, by mid-2009 many major American and British banks had recovered their nerve, simultaneously demanding government austerity and promising their staff yet more bonuses. But the greater profits reported by stronger banks such as Goldman's, JPMorgan, Barclays and HSBC derived both from the elimination of rivals that had gone bust and from massive state support (for example, access to virtually free money from the central banks). George Soros described the banks' profits as 'gifts . . . from the government'.[152] Kenneth Rogoff, former chief economist of the IMF, accused the US authorities of 'looking the other way while banks gamble under the umbrella of taxpayer guarantees'.[153] This state of affairs is tribute to the political power of banking capital highlighted, as we have seen, by another former occupant of the same post, Simon Johnson. But the state-engineered banking recovery was not necessarily evidence of a wider economic upsurge.

These developments have caused much concern on the free-market right. Niall Ferguson has even argued that they have 'provided a belated vindication' of Hilferding's and Lenin's predictions of the rise of 'State Monopoly Capitalism'.[154] Willem Buiter attacks the bank bailouts for creating 'moral hazard': in other words, confident that the state will rescue them if things go wrong, bankers have no incentive to avoid extreme risk-taking. Buiter argues that states should be prepared to let banks so bust.[155] The logic of this argument is that a large-scale clearout will leave behind it a population of capitals that are efficient and profitable. Here we find ourselves at the other horn of the dilemma that faces contemporary capitalism. In September 2008 the US Treasury Secretary, Hank Paulson, decided to let Lehman Brothers go bust, in part because of legal difficulties facing a rescue, in part, according to the *Financial Times*, for the kind of reason advanced by Buiter: 'Mr Paulson does not wish to fuel any further a growing bailout culture in the US, which has already led the troubled automotive industry to seek billions of dollars in loan guarantees.'[156] The result was the most severe global financial crash since October 1929, which at the very least helped push the world economy into a severe recession. For once words didn't wholly fail George W. Bush when he pleaded with Congressional leaders to pass the $700bn bailout plan ten days after the Lehman collapse that had forced a reversal of Paulson's earlier stance: 'If money isn't loos-

ened up, this sucker could go down.'[157] Allowing unprofitable firms to go to the wall might lead to the large-scale
devaluation of capital needed to restore the rate of profit
to levels that would launch a wave of sustained accumulation, but it might do so only through a prolonged depression as deep as that of the 1930s. The 1937–8 recession
underlines the protracted character of that slump, which
was only broken as states launched the rearmament programmes that pitched the world out of the frying pan of
depression into the fire of war.

Capitalism is thus stuck in a structural dilemma: if the
leading states let the market do its worst and sweep away
inefficient capitals, the result may be a prolonged slump;
but if they prevent the wholesale devaluation of capital,
the long-term crisis of overaccumulation and profitability
will continue. The existence of this dilemma doesn't mean
that there will be no recovery: the effects of fiscal stimuli
and firms' need to rebuild their inventories will lead to a
renewal of economic growth. But any recovery will develop
against the background of deep and unresolved structural
problems. These are not simply the overhang of unprofitable capital; as I argue in the following chapter, there is
little sign that the unbalanced and unstable interdependence of the US and China will cease to be the main motor
of the world economy. By the autumn of 2009 Nouriel
Roubini was one of many commentators arguing that a
new financial bubble had developed, in his view fuelled by
the availability of ultra-cheap money thanks to zero interest rates and the weakness of the dollar, and centred on
the 'emerging market' economies of the South.[158] The economic and financial crisis of the late 2000s was not an
accident nor the mere result of a banking system that had
escaped control. It was a moment of revelation, one that
exposed the systemic contradictions with which global
capitalism has been struggling for decades.

– 2 –
Empire Confined

The state roars back

Whatever else it may have done, the global economic and financial crisis has pretty definitively settled one of the dullest debates of the past two decades. One of the chief 'follies of globalization theory', as Justin Rosenberg admirably put it, was the idea that greater global economic integration has fatally weakened the nation state. Various theoretical constructions were erected by scholars, and faithfully maintained by armies of journalists and students, seeking to demonstrate the marginalization of the nation-state and its replacement by what liberals called 'global governance', and Toni Negri and Michael Hardt on the radical left described as the transnational network power of 'Empire'. The capacity of financial markets to operate across borders, the power of capital flows to make or break national economies, were cited as prime reasons for the decline of the nation-state.[1]

The financial crash blew these constructions apart. It certainly demonstrated the destructive power of cross-border flows. But as the banking system crumbled and the world slipped into recession, it was the state that came to the rescue with nationalizations, bailouts and fiscal stimuli. George Friedman, who through his strategic intelligence website Stratfor expounds a somewhat eccentric but often perceptive version of the realist view of international relations, puts it very well:

> what is most important is to see the manner in which state power surged in the summer and fall of 2008. The balance of power between business and the state, always dynamic, underwent a profound change, with the power of the state surging and the power of business contracting. Power was not in the hands of Lehman Brothers or Barclays. It was in the hands of Washington and London. At the same time, the power of the nation surged as the importance of multilateral organizations and sub-national groups declined. The nation-state roared back to life after it had seemed to be drifting into irrelevance.[2]

As Friedman points out, the persisting power of nation-states was central to both the crises of late summer and early autumn 2008 – the war between Russia and Georgia as well as the financial crash. That war was waged by Moscow essentially to halt its encirclement by the North Atlantic Treaty Organization (NATO), a US-led multilateral organization. The weakness of the NATO response to the war was not simply a consequence of the US entanglement in western Asia. In effect, Dimitri Medvedev and Vladimir Putin, uneasy partners at the head of the Russian state, played what one might call the Rumsfeld card, splitting NATO. In the lead-up to the invasion of Iraq in March 2003, Donald Rumsfeld, the US Defense Secretary, famously dismissed French and German opposition as 'old Europe. If you look at the entire NATO Europe today, the centre of gravity is shifting east.'[3] In February 2003 ten east and central European governments signed a statement drafted by Bruce Jackson, an ex-US military intelligence officer, that supported war on Iraq.[4] What the Georgian war, in the dying days of a now humbled Bush administration, showed was that more than one could play that game. In this case, the central and east European states were much more directly engaged than they were over Iraq, since they see membership of the European Union and NATO as a package offering both admission to the liberal capitalist club and a security guarantee against Russia. After the Georgian war, they were joined in their denunciations of Moscow and demands for NATO solidarity with Georgia and Ukraine, predictably enough, by Britain. Poland rushed to sign a highly unpopular missile defence deal with the US.

But the leading continental powers, France and Germany, took a very different line. They had already vetoed NATO membership action plans for Ukraine and Georgia in April 2008. Now they ensured that NATO and EU summits after the war confined themselves to words and not deeds. Even Silvio Berlusconi's right-wing government in Italy, which had been initially gung-ho over Iraq, took a soft line over Georgia. The reasons for this stance were thoroughly ignoble, but the most important of them – the EU's growing energy dependence on Russia – isn't going to change any time soon. European natural gas production is projected to fall to half its 2006 level by 2020. Russia has the world's largest natural gas reserves. It's not rocket science to predict that the contribution of Russian gas to European consumption is going to rise above its current level of around 25 per cent. Simon Blakey of Cambridge Energy Research Associates told the *Financial Times*: 'The scale of the interdependence is so huge it is really not possible to make a major difference to it even over the space of two decades.'[5]

The same pattern of diverging national interests was revealed by the EU's response to the financial crash. After all, the EU was the most important exhibit for the theorists of state decline, who argued it was displacing national sovereignty with a 'multiscalar' system of governance rising from the municipality and region through the nation-state to the level of the Community itself. And, whatever difficulties the EU might have had in getting its geopolitical act together, it was undeniably a success economically, with the great recent landmarks of the launch of the single internal market in 1992, the introduction of the euro in 1999, and the remarkably smooth accession of ten new member states, mainly in eastern and central Europe, in 2004. Yet the EU response to the financial crash was little short of shambolic. The most spectacular instance came in the immediate aftermath of the panic caused by the Lehman collapse. On 4 October 2008, the heads of the four most powerful European governments – those of Britain, France, Germany and Italy – met in Paris at the invitation of President Nicolas Sarkozy. They agreed on little concrete, but they did condemn the decision of the southern Irish government, faced with the threat of a bank run, to offer an unlimited guarantee of all deposits – a move that might undermine banks based elsewhere where the state had not given the same blanket protection to savers. No sooner had she returned to Berlin than the German Chancellor, Angela Merkel, announced a similar guarantee for all private deposits.

A subsequent summit of the euro-zone governments (also attended by Gordon Brown, the British Prime Minister) on 12 October did reassure the markets with a greater display of coherence. A €1,873bn package was agreed on to prop the banks up. But these measures – and a subsequent €200bn fiscal stimulus endorsed at the EU's December summit – were deceptive. Even though announced within the framework of the EU or the euro-zone, they were an agglomeration of national initiatives rather than a coordinated programme. Wolfgang Munchau, a *Financial Times* columnist who has been a consistent critic of the ineffectiveness of the EU response, lambasted the German government in particular for its complacency, even comparing Merkel to Heinrich Brüning, the German Chancellor in 1930–2, who responded to the Great Depression by cutting spending and raising taxes and thereby helped to pave the way for Hitler.[6] The extraordinary decision of the Bundestag in May 2009 to adopt a constitutional amendment requiring states to maintain balanced budgets and limiting the federal deficit to 0.35 per cent of national income suggests Munchau may not have been exaggerating. Meanwhile, EU member states came up with their own measures to rescue favoured industrial firms: thus in February 2009 the French government promised €6bn in preferential loans to Renault and Peugeot-Citroën in return for pledges that no car factories would be closed in France. Axel Webber, President of the Bundesbank, accused the European Commission, supposedly the guardian of the internal market, of encouraging this renationalization of economic policy by pushing banks in receipt of state aid to cut down their cross-border lending.[7] Munchau went further, warning that the rescues and stimulus packages, because of their national focus, were simultaneously ineffectual and undermining the single market.[8] For Joschka Fischer, the former German Foreign Minister, '[t]he global economic crisis is relentlessly laying bare [t]he EU's flaws and limitations. Without common economic and financial policies, co-ordinated at a minimum among euro-zone member states, the cohesion of European monetary union and the EU – indeed, their very existence – will be in unprecedented danger.'[9]

The most important of these flaws concerned economic and monetary union (EMU). This was, as the name suggests, an essentially *monetary* arrangement. The European Central Bank (ECB) issues the euro and manages the euro-zone's money supply and interest rates. From the very beginning of the financial crisis in August 2007 it intervened actively in European money markets to try to keep the banks afloat. But there was no fiscal equivalent of the ECB. The proportion of European national income taken by the EU is negligible. The power to tax, borrow and spend remains firmly with the member states. But, as we have seen, this was a crisis in which fiscal policy took centre-stage, both to recapitalize the insolvent banks and to compensate for the fall in effective demand with greater government borrowing and spending. There were good

political reasons for this structural discrepancy: despite the
neoliberal desire to harness the dangerous fiscal powers of
the state, it was in part precisely the much greater democratic legitimacy of the member states as opposed to that
of the European Council, Commission and even Parliament that allowed them to retain control over fiscal policy.
At the time of EMU, some critics had argued that a purely
monetary union would prove unsustainable unless but-
tressed by a federal political union. The EU's feeble and
uncoordinated response to the financial crisis suggested
that this critique might be right for economic reasons. As
Friedman put it,

> In the end, power did not reside with Europe, but rather
> with its individual countries. It wasn't Brussels that was
> implementing decisions made in Strasbourg; the centres of
> power were in Paris, London, Rome, Berlin and the other
> capitals of Europe and the world. Power devolved back to
> the states that governed nations. Or, to be more precise,
> the twin crises revealed that power had never left there.[10]

If this diagnosis bears any relation to the truth, then the
EU is caught in a tight bind. For if its lack of democratic
legitimacy means it lacks the power effectively to respond
to the global economic and financial crisis, it is very hard
to see how it can in the short term acquire the necessary
authority to overcome this weakness. On the contrary, the
gulf between the economic and political elites of neoliberal
Europe and the mass of citizens has been demonstrated in
a succession of popular votes – above all, the defeat of the
European Constitutional Treaty by referendums in France
and the Netherlands in May 2005 and of the repackaged
Lisbon Reform Treaty in the southern Irish referendum of
June 2008. Even if the devastating impact of the crisis in
Ireland – one of the countries where the credit bubble was
most distended – eventually helped to scare voters into
endorsing the Reform Treaty in a restaged referendum, it
is clear that there is no real political base for a move

towards a more federal EU. Accordingly, ultimate power
will continue to reside in the member states with their
diverging, sometimes conflicting interests.

The retreat from economic globalization, though most
marked in Europe, was a general trend. According to the
Bank for International Settlements, cross-border lending
by banks shrank by $4,800bn to $31,000bn in the nine
months to December 2008, the sharpest fall on record. For
the *Financial Times*, '[t]he pullback represents the reversal
of years of financial globalisation, fuelled by a sharp
increase in so-called "home bias" as bankers tried to
reduce risk while maintaining domestic lending to please
the national governments that were acting as their guaran-
tors of last resort'.[11] The World Bank pointed out in March
2009 that after the G20 had at their emergency summit
on 15 November 2008 promised to avoid protectionist
measures, states, including seventeen members of the G20,
had implemented no less than forty-seven measures
designed to give their firms a competitive advantage in
global trade. Tariff increases amounted to only a third of
the measures, and were adopted mainly by developing
countries. Export subsidies were more common. For
example, the United States, France, Germany, Britain,
Canada, China, Brazil, Argentina, Sweden and Italy all
provided direct or indirect financial support to their car
industries. Most notoriously, the US Congress inserted
into Barack Obama's initial fiscal stimulus package a 'Buy
American' requirement on any recipients of state support,
whose effects (despite the administration's efforts to water
the clause down) provoked a wave of boycotts of American goods by Canadian municipalities.[12] In an effort to
boost exports, China let its currency drift down on the
foreign exchanges, provoking an angry reaction from the
Obama team.

This protectionist drift came against the background of
the comprehensive failure of the World Trade Organization to complete the Doha road of trade liberalization
talks, mainly because of persistent conflicts between the

US and the EU on the one hand and the most powerful of the so-called emerging market economies such as China, India and Brazil on the other. These developments were particularly alarming for those raised in the neoliberal folklore that the decisive factor in transforming the Wall Street financial crisis of October 1929 into the Great Depression was the passage by the US Congress of the Smoot-Hawley Act, which sharply raised tariffs, in June 1930, even though, by then, as Christopher Dow puts it, 'the depression was already severe'.[13] But the present economic and financial crisis is unlikely to lead to the kind of disintegration of the world market into protectionist blocs, accompanied by the contraction of international trade by two thirds, that took place in 1929–33. Economic globalization has involved, not merely the expansion and international integration of financial markets, but also the development of much more extensive transnational production networks. Any serious unravelling of these networks would lead to a catastrophic economic contraction that it is in the interests of all states to strive to avoid.

The significance of the real but weaker forms of 'deglobalization' generated by the present crisis is different. In the first place, as Friedman argues, it represents a shift in the balance of power between the state and capital. Banks in particular have been forced to turn to their national governments to rescue them, and are likely, as a result, to find their activities considerably more restricted in future. This change will be reinforced if it is accompanied by the reduction in the relative size of the overblown financial sector that has been widely predicted, particularly in the US and Britain, where process of financialization went furthest (in 2007 three million people were employed in manufacturing in the UK, and 6.5 million in financial services).[14] As we have seen, firms in other sectors (notably the car industry) have also turned to the state for support. The internationalization of capital makes the resulting relationships often very complex. The bank rescues have sometimes involved pumping money into foreign banks:

as buyers of AIG credit default swaps, Société Générale received $11.9bn from the American government, Deutsche Bank $11.8bn, Barclays $8.5bn, and BNP Paribas $4.9bn.[15] The US and France have concentrated on rescuing their national car firms. This is not so simple for, say, Britain and even Germany, hosts to foreign car multinationals (which completely dominate the sector in Britain). Thus the rival bids by Fiat, Magna and RHJ to take over the European subsidiaries of General Motors were complicated by the insistence of the German government that there should be no closures in Germany of plants belonging to Opel, GM's German brand. Nevertheless, that the general trend is to strengthen the nation-state vis-à-vis capital seems undeniable, as is indicated by the fact that it was the German government, thanks to its readiness to offer loan guarantees, that temporarily became the arbiter of GM Europe's fate (before Detroit, its financial position strengthened by the widely adopted state-subsidized cash-for-clunkers schemes, decided to torpedo the sale).

Secondly, and partly because of the connections binding particular states and capitals together, the divergent interests of nation-states make efforts at international coordination difficult at precisely the time at which they are needed. Thus take the case of Germany: Berlin's resistance to Barack Obama's proposals for an internationally coordinated fiscal stimulus is not simply a matter of folk memories of the hyper-inflations of the early 1920s and late 1940s. Through a process of corporate restructuring and wage-repression, reinforced by the previous Red-Green government's Agenda 2010 programme of making labour markets more flexible, Germany succeeded by the mid-2000s in re-establishing itself as the world's biggest export economy. In 2008 exports made up 47 per cent of GDP, compared to less than 20 per cent in Japan and 13 per cent in the US. This high level of export dependence explains Germany's extreme vulnerability to the sharp decline in international trade in 2008–9. The *Financial Times* glossed the approach Merkel outlined in an interview with the paper in the spring of 2009 thus: 'sit out the crisis, preserving industrial strength as much as possible, and await the eventual upturn. The reliance on exports "is not something you can change in two years", Ms Merkel said. "It is not something we even want to change." '[16] A less charitable interpretation might be that Germany's strategy came down to free-riding on fiscal expansion elsewhere, and thereby displacing the costs, in greater government borrowing and lost export markets, onto other states. Michael Glos, the German Economics Minister, unblushingly avowed in November 2008: 'We can only hope that the measures taken by other countries . . . will help our export economy.'[17]

Free-riding is a collective action problem. In other words, it is an example of how the pursuit by actors of their individual interests may block an outcome that would benefit them all. Both liberals and Marxists have seen the state as a way of solving collective action problems. In the Marxist version, the role of the capitalist state is partly to impose on individual capitals policies that are in their general interest but that each capital on its own finds it too costly to undertake.[18] But what the present crisis has underlined is that no institutions capable of performing this function exist at the European, let alone the global level. Nor simply do the existing forms of 'global governance' lack the powers of coercion and extraction that are among the defining features of states, but the crisis is likely to leave these powers more firmly entrenched at the nation-state level. For Friedman, all this is a reaffirmation of the eternal verities of realism:

> The world is a very different place from what it was in the spring of 2008. Or, to be more precise, it is a much more traditional place than many thought. It is a world of nations pursuing their own interests and collaborating where they choose. Those interests are economic, political and military, and they are part of a single fabric. The illusion of multilateralism was not put to rest – it will never

die – but it was certainly put to bed. It is a world we can readily recognize from history.[19]

Others may find this less reassuring. After all, the speed with which first financial instability and then recession spread across national borders in 2007–9 demonstrates just how integrated the world economy has become. Much more international coordination is *needed*. The trouble is that this world economy is organized within the framework of a constitutively unstable capitalist economic system *and* a political system of sovereign states. Despite the real forms of transnational cooperation that exist, anarchy continues to reign, both economically and politically. As Adair Turner succinctly puts it, 'the world has a global economy but not a global government'.[20] Once again, from a Marxist perspective, there is nothing particularly new or surprising about this. After the First World War the Communist International highlighted the contradiction between the global development of the productive forces under capitalism and the division of the world into nation-states. Trotsky wrote in the manifesto of its founding congress in 1919: 'The national state which gave a mighty impulsion to capitalist development has become too narrow for the further development of productive forces.'[21] This contradiction now seems particularly acute.

One way in which the Marxist tradition has sought to capture the anarchy that reigns under capitalism is through the theory of imperialism. As David Harvey and I have both argued, capitalist imperialism is to be understood as the intersection of economic and geopolitical competition. In other words, it is what happens when the competitive struggles among firms fuse, often in a complex and conflictual form, with the geopolitical rivalries between states.[22] As we have already seen, 2008 was marked by a significant shift in the latter. Let's turn to consider this, and to weigh the broader geopolitical consequences of the economic and financial crisis.

Collision of empires

Probably the best place to start is with the global project of the administration of the younger Bush, since in many ways its disastrous failure defines contemporary world politics. The project can best be seen as a radicalization of the approaches of the administrations of the elder Bush and Bill Clinton. All three sought, in a global conjuncture defined by both a redistribution of relative economic power mainly favouring the East Asian states and by the collapse of the Soviet Union, to entrench the hegemony of the United States by maintaining and extending the institutionalized system of interstate cooperation constructed by Washington after the Second World War. Under George W. Bush the US went further in the direction already taken by preceding administrations by seeking to exploit in a more unilateralist and aggressive way than Bush *père* or Clinton had done America's two main comparative advantages, namely the Pentagon and the dollar. Thus the Bush administration sought to use the overwhelming conventional military superiority of the US to expand and consolidate its dominance of western Asia, thereby reinforcing Washington's ability to control access to the huge energy reserves of the region. At the same time, it tried to increase the competitiveness of American firms and help to revive the US economy after the 2000–1 recession by letting the dollar float downwards against other currencies. Both these initiatives were underpinned by Bretton Woods II – in other words, by the economic circuit through which a large chunk of the foreign revenues of the big export economies was lent back to the US, helping to finance Washington's twin budget and balance of payments deficits.[23]

It is fair to say that this entire enterprise has been a pretty comprehensive failure. In particular the inability of the US rapidly to transform Iraq into a pliant neoliberal client state has been a geopolitical catastrophe. The Iraq adventure produced what even neoconservatives acknowledge to be a crisis of legitimacy for the US.[24] Moreover, it created a black hole that absorbed American military capabilities and thereby limited Washington's options elsewhere, for example, helping to create the space in which left governments could take and hold office across a very large swathe of Latin America. The Bush administration could claim to have brought a degree of stability to Iraq after the first disastrous three and a half years of the occupation. This was less a consequence of the famous surge in US troop numbers in 2007–8, than because of two sets of political deals. The first was with Iran, the regional power that has been strengthened by the overthrow of Saddam Hussein, and with the Shia parties aligned with Iran that dominate Nouri al-Maliki's client government. The second was with Sunni resistance groups that initially fought the occupation but were willing to ally themselves with the Americans for a mixture of money and protection against both the Maliki government and the sectarian fanatics of al-Qaida.

The problem with this strategy is obvious. The US currently holds the ring between two sets of allies who are deeply hostile to each other. Its ability to keep this ramshackle arrangement together is likely to deteriorate over time – particularly because Maliki was able to force the Bush administration to agree, very reluctantly, to the withdrawal of the bulk of American troops by the end of 2011. But even before Bush left office the Sunni 'Awakening' movement was complaining that the Maliki government was persecuting its supporters and refusing to honour American promises to find them jobs in the client army and police. Meanwhile, Moqtada al-Sadr's Mehdi Army, which combines the support of the Shia poor and opposition to the occupation, remained silent, awaiting its opportunity. Thomas Ricks, in a book devoted to the surge that is highly sympathetic to its main architect, General David Petraeus, now chief of US Central Command, concedes:

Yet it is unclear in 2009 if he did more than lengthen the war. In revising the US approach to the Iraq war, Petraeus found tactical success – that is, improved security – but not the clear political breakthrough that would have meant unambiguous strategic success. At the end of the surge, the fundamental political problems facing Iraq were the same ones as when it began. At the end of 2008, two years into the revamped war, there was no prospect of the fighting ending anytime soon. But it was almost certain that whenever it did end, it wouldn't be with the victory that the Bush administration continued to describe, of an Iraq that was both a stable democracy and an ally of the United States. Nor was that really the goal any more, though no one said so publicly. Under Petraeus, the American goal of transforming Iraq had been quietly scaled down. But even his less ambitious target of sustainable security would remain elusive, with no certainty of reaching it anytime soon.[25]

What Friedman calls the 'twin crises' of 2008 inflicted further damage on the Bush project. In the first place, the administration generated yet more blowback – not as spectacular as 9/11, but potentially as serious – by provoking a confrontation with Russia in the Caucasus. One key dimension of US grand strategy since the end of the Cold War has been ruthlessly to exploit Russia's weakness by expanding the EU and NATO into eastern and central Europe as a way of both encircling Russia and expanding American influence deep into Eurasia. Begun under Clinton in the 1990s, the policy was extended by the Bush administration, which gave enthusiastic support to the rather shaky pro-Western regimes in Ukraine and Georgia. Exploiting Russian weakness may have seemed like a low-cost policy during the disarray and disintegration of Boris Yeltsin's presidency in the 1990s. Russia under Putin and Medvedev is an altogether different proposition. The Russian economy was a major beneficiary of the energy boom of the mid-2000s. Putin re-established effective political control over the oil and gas industries. He brought order to the Russian state, rebuilt its military capabilities, and promoted a kind of authoritarian capitalism ideologically central to which is a strident nationalism committed as far as possible to reversing the collapse of the Soviet empire.

In any circumstances seeking to expand NATO to incorporate Ukraine and Georgia, in two of Russia's key border zones, would have been reckless. Given the shift in relative power between Washington and Moscow, the policy – strongly pushed by Bush at the NATO summit in Bucharest in April 2008 – was the height of folly. In their confrontation with Georgia, the Russians could count on three decisive advantages. First, they had overwhelming local military superiority. Second, any attempt by the US to respond militarily – which would have been required if Georgia had been a member of NATO – would have risked a general war. It is highly improbable that even Bush and his belligerent Vice-President, Dick Cheney, were ready to wage a thermonuclear war over Georgia. In any case, such a large proportion of US military capabilities was tied up in Iraq and Afghanistan that Washington's options were hugely restricted. It shouldn't be forgotten that, in the most dangerous confrontation of the Cold War, the Cuban missile crisis of October 1962, the US enjoyed massive local conventional superiority. Third, as we have already seen, Putin and Medvedev could play the same game of divide-and-rule expertly practised by Washington in both Western Europe and Asia long before Rumsfeld invoked the divide between 'New' and 'Old' Europe. Moreover, the EU's growing dependence on Russian energy gives Moscow a long-term advantage, by enabling it to divide Washington's European allies and thereby to undermine the ability of the US to brigade them together in a new East–West confrontation.

The war in Georgia, like the occupation of Iraq, demonstrated the limits of US imperial power, but they did so in different ways. Iraq reaffirmed an ancient truth, namely that even the greatest military power can be defeated when it is confronted by an insurgent population among whom it has little political support. But the experience

nevertheless fitted into the *doxa* of the post-Cold War era
– that warfare would now be predominantly asymmetric,
pitting states against non-state adversaries such as the
allegedly centre-less al-Qaida network. What NATO
expansion ran up against in Georgia was the resistant
power of another state – of Russia asserting its centuries-
old interest in securing a zone of influence around its
borders. The episode was widely seen as symptomatic of
the limits, not just of US military reach, but of the transnational liberal-capitalist space that Washington has constructed and steadily expanded over the past seven decades.

Consider, for example, the projected global power-shift
mapped out by the US National Intelligence Council (NIC)
in November 2008:

> In terms of size, speed, and directional flow, the transfer
> of *global wealth and economic power* now under way –
> roughly from West to East – is without precedent in
> modern history. This shift derives from two sources. First,
> increases in oil and commodity prices have generated
> windfall profits for the Gulf states and Russia. Second,
> lower costs combined with government policies have
> shifted the locus of manufacturing and some service indus-
> tries to Asia.[26]

As much as effecting a shift in the distribution of economic
power, these changes also limited the global reach of
Western liberal capitalism:

> With some notable exceptions like India, the states that are
> beneficiaries of the massive shift of wealth – China, Russia,
> and Gulf States – are non-democratic and their economic
> policies blur distinctions between public and private. These
> states are not following the Western liberal model for
> self-development but are using a different model – 'state
> capitalism'.[27]

From this perspective, the Georgian war represented the
historical moment at which state capitalism bit back. But

it would be a mistake to see this as the start a new cold war. Russia's relative power has declined significantly over the long term, even if it has revived somewhat recently. The USSR emerged from the Second World War as the biggest land power in Eurasia. By the 1970s it had a massive thermonuclear arsenal and the capability to project conventional military power globally. As recently as 1980, the Soviet Union produced 14.8 per cent of global manufacturing output, nearly half the US share of 31.5 per cent. In 2007, on the most favourable measure of national income (purchasing power parity), Russia accounted for 3.2 per cent of world gross domestic product, less than its 1992 share of 4.2 per cent, and way below the US share of 21.63 per cent. The highest estimate of Russian military spending put it at $70bn in 2006, compared to the Pentagon's $535.9bn.[28] Russia has lost strategically and economically vital territory in Ukraine and Central Asia, and its population continues to decline. It is also vulnerable because of its much greater integration in global markets than during the Soviet era. The Georgian war began a significant flight of capital from Russia, partly caused by a local version of the global credit crunch that diminished the fortunes of Russia's super-rich as tumbling share prices undermined the often massive loans they had taken out. The Russian economy was also hit by the precipitate fall of the oil price from the high it reached in July 2008.

But these weaknesses should be put in perspective. The gap between Washington's and Moscow's economic and military capabilities is indeed far greater than it was during the Cold War. This means that the US is the only genuinely global power. So it has to spread its resources much more widely than any other state and hence is vulnerable to what Paul Kennedy famously called 'imperial overstretch'.[29] It is precisely such a crisis, arising from American entanglement in western Asia, that Russia has been able to exploit. Moscow still has very formidable military capabilities that have been renewed thanks to the energy bonanza. It demonstrated in Georgia both its capacity and its will to assert its own imperial interests along its borders. Russia may not be able to compete with the US globally, but it can contest Washington's influence in several important regions, particularly those that are critical energy suppliers – certainly the Caucasus and Central Asia and potentially the Middle East as well.

The financial crash was a further blow to US hegemony. It inflicted another immense symbolic setback after the Iraq catastrophe: supposedly ascendant Anglo-American capitalism blew itself up, taking the world down with it. Francis Fukuyama, whose announcement in 1989 of the End of History was a neoconservative affirmation of the ideological power of what he now calls the 'American brand' of free-market capitalism and liberal democracy, mournfully acknowledged the reverse:

> It's hard to fathom just how badly these signature features of the American brand have been discredited. Between 2002 and 2007, while the world was enjoying an unprecedented period of growth, it was easy to ignore those European socialists and Latin American populists who denounced the US economic model as 'cowboy capitalism'. But now the engine of that growth, the American economy, has gone off the rails and threatens to drag the rest of the world down with it. Worse, the culprit is the American model itself: under the mantra of less government, Washington failed to adequately regulate the financial sector and allowed it to do tremendous harm to the rest of the society. Democracy was tarnished even earlier. Once Saddam was proved not to have WMD [weapons of mass destruction], the Bush administration sought to justify the Iraq War by linking it to a broader 'freedom agenda'; suddenly the promotion of democracy was a chief weapon in the war against terrorism. To many people around the world, America's rhetoric about democracy sounds a lot like an excuse for furthering US hegemony.[30]

But the economic and financial crises also reduced US power more directly and materially. Dealing with it would take Washington's attention away from other issues and drain away yet more of its political energy and economic resources. American isolationism during the 1930s can't be reduced to popular fears of another world war and the parochialism and xenophobia of many members of Congress; it also reflected the Roosevelt administration's absorption in trying to fix the US economy.[31] More directly, the huge injections of government money by the Bush and Obama administrations to rescue the banks and avert a new depression would inevitably mean a huge increase in US borrowing, above all from the East Asian states that, as we saw in Chapter 1, have been financing the American deficit. This would affect the US position in the state system in various ways. Worrying about the cost of the bank bailout in the immediate aftermath of the Lehman collapse, Kenneth Rogoff, former chief economist of the International Monetary Fund, wrote in a passage that shows the clear understanding the American establishment has of the underpinnings of its global power and of the interrelations between them: 'A large expansion in debt will impose enormous fiscal costs on the US, ultimately hitting growth through a combination of higher taxes and lower spending. It will certainly make it harder for the US to maintain its military dominance, which has been one of the linchpins of the dollar.'[32]

Greater American foreign borrowing is likely to put increasing strain on the relationship between the US and China. In early 2009, Brad Setser of the Council on Foreign Relations estimated China's foreign reserves amounted to $2,300bn, of which about $1,700bn was invested in dollar assets. In 2008 China lent the US more than $400bn – equivalent to more than 10 per cent of Chinese gross domestic product. China owned nearly $700bn worth of US Treasury bonds ($3,300bn worth of US Treasuries are owned by foreign investors, more than half of the total). The financial crisis, and the fear that the US would resort to its time-honoured tactic of trying to revive the economy by devaluing the dollar, made Chinese officials considerably more assertive, and openly critical of American policies. The Bush administration's decision in September 2008 to rescue the semi-public mortgage giants Freddie Mae and Fannie Mac is reputed to have been partly prompted by Chinese sales of the firm's bonds in favour of US Treasuries. But Luo Ping, a senior official of the China Banking Regulatory Commission, told a conference in New York in February 2009: 'US Treasuries are the safe haven; it is the only option. Once you start issuing $1–$2 trillion . . . we know the dollar is going to depreciate, so we hate you guys, but there is nothing much we can do.'[33] The Chinese Prime Minister, Wen Jiabao, was more diplomatic when he addressed the National People's Congress the following month, but the message was unmistakable: 'We have lent a huge amount of money to the United States. Of course we are concerned about the safety of our assets. To be honest, I am a little bit worried. I request the US to maintain its good credit, to honour its promises and to guarantee the safety of China's assets.'[34] These remarks followed the announcement by Tim Geithner, Obama's Treasury Secretary, during his Senate confirmation hearings that January, that 'President Obama – backed by the conclusions of a broad range of economists – believes that China is manipulating its currency' – an assertion that the new administration did not subsequently repeat, perhaps because it had been warned not to insult its chief creditor.

The impact on the state system of this shift in relative power, and the longer term trends it reinforces are being registered by American planners. Whereas the NIC's 2003 twenty-year forward projections had assumed continuing US dominance in 2020, its November 2008 report painted a very different picture:

> The *international system* – as constructed following the Second World War – will be almost unrecognizable by 2025 owing to the rise of emerging powers, a globalizing economy, an historic transfer of relative wealth and eco-

nomic power from West to East, and the growing influence of non-state actors. By 2025, the international system will be a *global multipolar one* with gaps in national power continuing to narrow between developed and developing countries . . . the next 20 years of transition to a new system are fraught with risks. Strategic rivalries are most likely to revolve around trade, investments, and technological innovation and acquisition, but we cannot rule out a 19th century-like scenario of arms races, territorial expansion, and military rivalries . . . Although the United States is likely to remain the single most powerful actor, the United States' relative strength – even in the military realm – will decline and US leverage will become more constrained.[35]

David Harvey argues that 'the tectonic shift away from United States dominance and hegemony' that the NIC report predicts confirms Giovanni Arrighi's long-standing thesis that American hegemony is nearing its end.[36] This judgement dovetails with my own argument that the end of the Cold War did not mark the ascent of an American super-imperialism but rather the beginning of an era of more intense geopolitical competition and greater global instability.[37] But tectonic shifts are long-term processes: even if geopolitical changes don't take the millions of years of geological history, the precise pace at which they unfold is often hard to predict. Hence the debate among International Relations specialists about why the emergence of a temporarily unipolar state system at the end of the Cold War did not lead rapidly to states balancing against the US, as structural realist theory would predict.[38] In the light of these considerations, it is important to consider the weight of forces counteracting a rapid eclipse of American hegemony.

One of these – the economic and financial crisis itself – is highlighted by Niall Ferguson in an imaginary history of 2009 written at the end of the previous year:

the troubles of the rest of the world meant that in relative terms the US gained, politically as well as economically.

Many commentators had warned in 2008 that the financial crisis would be the final nail in the coffin of American credibility around the world . . . Yet this was to overlook two things. The first was that most other economic systems fared even worse than America's when the crisis struck: the country's fiercest critics – Russia, Venezuela – fell flattest. The second was the enormous boost to America's international reputation that followed Obama's inauguration.[39]

I'll return to Ferguson's second point, about the impact of Obama. The first is worth developing and unpacking a bit. As we saw in the previous chapter, the idea that the so-called 'emerging market economies' had 'decoupled' from the US and were capable of powering global economic growth was definitively disproved in 2008–9. The collapse of American domestic demand sucked the rest of the world into a deep economic slump. Martin Wolf is entirely right to say: 'The US, it is clear, remains the core of the world economy.'[40] Moreover, as we have also seen, the second and third biggest economies in the advanced capitalist world – Japan and Germany – have been even more severely affected by the recession because of their relatively high level of dependence on exports. As for the BRICs (Brazil, Russia, India and China), they are, as a category, little more than a broker's fantasy – the concept was invented by Goldman Sachs, whose growing investments in Chinese banks gives it a definite interest in talking up the prospects especially of China. The economies grouped together under the category are in fact quite heterogeneous. Brazil and Russia are both highly dependent on raw-material exports and therefore are vulnerable to the kind of sharp fall in commodity prices that was induced by the global recession of 2008–9. As for India, though it has a significant manufacturing base, its economic rise was largely a consequence of a specialization in services facilitated by the trend for Northern transnational corporations to offshore some of their activities. As Fareed Zakaria puts it, '[i]f there ever was a race between India and China, it's over. China's economy is three times the size of India's and is still growing at a faster clip. The law of compounding tells us that India can overtake China only if there are drastic and sustained shifts in both countries' trajectories that last for decades.'[41]

The real challenge to US hegemony doesn't come from the nebulous BRICs, but from China. In the past few years, its economy has overtaken Britain and Germany. In all probability it will soon – perhaps as a result of the impact of the present crisis on relative growth rates – supplant Japan as the second largest economy in the world, though still a long way behind the US. There is indeed a case for saying that, if the crisis may have enhanced the relative economic power of the US vis-à-vis some of its rivals, China too may emerge stronger. We have already seen one respect in which that is true, namely the growing financial dependence of the US on China. Moreover, although China's export-geared economy was hit by the slump in world trade in 2008–9, it was less severely affected than other big manufacturing and trading economies: the economy grew at a slower rate, but didn't shrink. Assuming one believes the figures (there are many doubts about the reliability of Chinese national-income statistics), according to Barclays Capital, China accounted for the entire rise in global output in the second quarter of 2009.[42] This performance is probably a result of the intense efforts by the Chinese state to counter recessionary tendencies. A mammoth $590bn fiscal stimulus was announced in November 2008 (although only about a quarter of that was estimated to be genuinely new money – the rest consisted mainly of planned investments that were brought forward to stimulate demand).[43] Perhaps more important, the state-controlled banking system was not significantly affected by the global financial crash. Rather than cut back on lending like their Western counterparts, the Chinese banks, on Beijing's instructions, lent $1,080bn in the first half of 2009 – though by the summer there were signs that this had inflated a new bubble in the Shanghai stock exchange.[44]

If, then, China's state-capitalist model held up relatively well in the economic storm unleashed by the financial crisis, there are nevertheless questions about its longer-term prospects. China's spectacular economic performance has depended on a stream of soft loans from state banks to private firms that have strong incentives to expand and export. As a consequence there are powerful tendencies towards overcapacity and low profitability.[45] As David McNally points out, evidence of a developing crisis of overaccumulation in China emerged before the onset of the credit crunch:

> the investment boom in China had exacerbated the problems of global overcapacity that first flared up in 1997. These began to manifest themselves in the Chinese economy from around 2005 on. According to the Chinese government's National Development and Reform Commission, China's steel industry had developed an annual capacity of 470 million metric tons at a time when actual output equalled only 350 million metric tons. This excess capacity of 120 million metric tons was greater than the *total* real output (112.5 million metric tons) of the world's second-largest steel producing country, Japan. Even worse problems of overaccumulation haunted the iron alloy industry, where capacity utilisation had slumped to a mere 40 per cent by 2005. And significant overcapacity plagued the auto, aluminium, cement and coke industries. Detailed studies suggested, for example, that by 2005 China's home appliance market had overcapacity rates of 30 per cent in washing machines, 40 per cent in refrigerators, 45 per cent in microwave ovens and a mind-blowing 87 per cent in televisions.[46]

One critical issue in mapping China's economic future concerns its ability to wean itself off its dependence on exports: exports make up 32.5 per cent of Chinese GDP.[47] Some economists argue that this dependence is exaggerated, since the actual value added in China to most exports is quite small because their production is a transnational process in which Chinese plants often contribute only the final assembly of complex parts imported from more advanced economies such as Germany, Japan and South Korea. Thus, according to one estimate, only 5 per cent of the $150 price of an iPod assembled in China is actually created there. But a study for the Hong Kong Monetary Authority concluded that, for every 10 per cent drop in exports, the GDP growth would fall by 2.5 percentage points.[48] In its dependence on exports, China shares a feature common to the other East Asian capitalisms (though it is unusual in being much more open to foreign direct investment than, say, Japan or South Korea). About 60 per cent of the final demand for Asian goods comes from the developed economies. The crisis has intensified calls for the 'rebalancing' of global demand in which the US in particular saves more and consumes less and China saves less and consumes more. 'There is no longer any choice for Asia', pontificates Clyde Prestowitz, of the Economic Strategy Institute. 'Asia has to start consuming more . . . The export-led model has outlived its usefulness.'[49]

Certainly, if China were to displace the US as the centre of the world economy, then it would need, not simply to continue growing at the spectacular rates of the past three decades, but greatly to expand domestic demand, which would provide a large market for the exports of other states. But the two requirements seem mutually inconsistent, since economic growth in China (and indeed the rest of East Asia), has depended on a high propensity to export. But, since productivity in China is much lower than in the US and other advanced economies, this means keeping wages low and thereby constraining the growth of the home market. Comparisons between China's development and that of the US are in some respects illuminating, inasmuch as they highlight shared characteristics such as a vast continental economy and the importance of local alliances between private entrepreneurs and political elites.[50] But the development of capitalism in China is significantly different inasmuch as it does not involve the large home market sustained by high wages and high productivity that is so distinctive of the US from its early years onwards. The 'export-led model' isn't just a matter of 'choice' but depends on deeply embedded constellations of class relations and interests that will be hard to change – as will, on the other side of the Pacific, the distinctive political economy that the US has developed since the early 1970s. China may indeed become the new centre of the world economy, but this is likely to be a much more complex, protracted and contested process than is suggested by those who engage in the mindless and often self-interested extrapolation of trends.

The implication of this analysis is that the US is likely to remain, by some distance, the biggest and most important capitalist economy for several decades to come. Its rulers continue to exploit the central position America occupies in the financial system. Thus in October 2008, in the wake of the crash, the Federal Reserve opened credit lines worth $30bn each to four key "emerging market" economies – Brazil, Mexico, Singapore and South Korea – effectively seeking to position itself as the global central bank. Washington also enjoys a significant advantage thanks to its institutionalized power in other regions. This is true both in Europe, where the weakness of the EU has been sharply exposed by the economic and financial crisis, and East Asia, where the rise of China has helped to lock Japan into its long-standing position of geopolitical subordination to the US. Indeed, the expansion of Chinese power in a region that also contains several important states – Japan, India, South Korea and, on the sidelines, Russia – gives the US considerable opportunities to continue practising divide-and-rule. This is, in effect, the general strategy that Zakaria commends to the US in a book, *The Post-American World*, that was apparently widely read by the Obama team:

> As China, India, Brazil, Russia, South Africa, and a host of smaller countries all do well in the years ahead, new

points of tension will emerge among them. Many of these rising countries have historical animosities, border disputes, and contemporary quarrels with one another; in most cases, nationalism will grow along with economic and geopolitical stature. Being a distant power, America is often a convenient partner for many regional nations worried about the rise of a hegemon in their midst. In fact, as the scholar William Wolforth notes, American influence is strengthened by the growth of a dominant regional power. These factors are often noted in discussions of Asia, but it is true of many other spots in the globe as well . . . these rivalries do give the United States an opportunity to play a large and constructive role at the centre of the global order. It has the potential to be what Bismarck helped Germany become (briefly) in the late nineteenth century – Europe's 'honest broker', forging close relationships with each of the major countries, ties that were closer than the ones those countries had with one another. It [Germany] was the hub of the European system. Being the global broker today would be a job involving not just the American government but its society, with all the strengths and perspectives that it will bring to the challenge. It is a role that the United States – with its global interests and presence, complete portfolio of power, and diverse immigrant communities – could learn to play with great skill.[51]

Orchestrating disharmony

And who better to pioneer this role as global broker than Barack Obama, embodying as he does in his own person the diversity of American society and its openness to the rest of the world? Slavoj Žižek has highlighted the immense and irreducible symbolic significance of Obama's election: 'The reason Obama's victory generated such enthusiasm is not only that, against all odds, it really happened: it demonstrated the possibility of such a thing happening.'[52] But, of necessity, the symbolic surplus incorporated in the person of Obama is ambiguous. He signifies that the frontiers of the possible are much broader than had previously been thought, thereby encouraging new emancipatory struggles. But he also represents valuable ideological capital to be used by the American state in rebuilding its global position after the disasters of George W. Bush's presidency.

The skill with which, after his inauguration, Obama moved to demonstrate his multilateralist credentials – for example, sending his Vice-President, Joe Biden, to the Munich Security Conference in February 2009 to promise a 'reset' of US–Russian relations, brokering a compromise between France and China at the G20 summit in April 2009, charming a Muslim audience at Cairo University that June – suggested a word-perfect performance of a script written by Zbigniew Brzezinski, the Democratic Party's most influential geopolitical thinker, and a vehement critic of the Bush administration for its failure to see that the US could best maintain its primacy in partnership with other powers, notably the EU.[53] But it is critical to understand that Obama's aim is precisely to preserve US hegemony, not elegantly to manage American decline. 'We will rebuild, we will recover, and the United States of America will emerge stronger than before', he told a Joint Session of Congress, which cheered his words to the rafters, in February 2009.[54]

Despite the discontinuity symbolized by Obama's accession to the presidency, what is most striking is the continuity between his administration and those of his two immediate predecessors. His senior staff was dispiritingly over-loaded with retreads from the Clinton era, headed by Hillary Rodham Clinton herself at the State Department. But more interesting were the continuities in policy between Barack Obama and George W. Bush. Here it is important to be precise. These continuities were not with the hubristic Bush team that proclaimed a global state of exception in September 2001 and invaded Iraq to remake the Middle East in March 2003, but with the chastened lame-duck administration hanging on to office after the Democratic victories in the mid-term Congressional elections of

November 2006. To some extent, this was dictated by the brute necessities of the economic and financial crisis. It was Hank Paulson, Bush's last Treasury Secretary, who largely set the agenda for Obama, Geithner and Lawrence Summers, chairman of the National Economic Council, with the series of emergency improvised measures he undertook in autumn 2008 – notably the part-nationalizations of bust institutions and the TARP (Troubled Assets Recovery Programme) bailout designed to buy time to rebuild the financial system. The fiscal stimulus undertaken by the new administration went further than most Republicans would have preferred, but both Reagan and Bush *fils* had shown themselves willing to exploit America's structural advantage deriving from the dollar's position in the international financial system to prime the pump by boosting military spending and cutting taxes for the rich. Obama also continued the policy, initiated by Bush, of making the G20 (which includes the leading states from the South) the main international forum for addressing the economic crisis.

The continuities were even starker in foreign policy. Withdrawal from Iraq – though one that would still leave a formidable US military presence in the country for 'training' purposes – had already been conceded by the Bush administration to the Maliki government. Pursuing diplomatic openings with Iran and Syria was certainly a shift from a Bush-Cheney administration that actively planned a military strike against the Tehran regime, but it was one of the main recommendations of the Iraq Study Group, an eminently bipartisan grouping of foreign policy sages headed by Jim Baker, arch-fixer of the Reagan and Bush Sr. administrations, that reported in December 2006. Obama made a concrete concession to Russia in September 2009, when he scrapped plans to base the US missile defence system in Poland and the Czech Republic. But this move (probably of little directly military significance) was followed a few weeks later by a speech by Biden in Romania rejecting Moscow's claims to a sphere of influence and calling for more pro-Western 'colour revolutions' like those in Georgia in 2003 and Ukraine in 2004. Obama also chose to order a surge in US troops in Afghanistan and continued to authorize air attacks on targets across the border in Pakistan and to press the Pakistani military to clamp down on jihadis, despite the evidence that the spreading war was both failing to defeat the Taliban and destabilizing Pakistan. A real change would come if the new administration, in order to revive the moribund and discredited Middle East 'peace process', and despite Obama's repeated professions of his unflinching commitment to Israel's security and refusal to condemn the assault on Gaza in the weeks before his inauguration, put pressure on Israel's most right-wing government to date to negotiate a deal that might give the Palestinians the facsimile (not, of course, the reality) of their own state. But, on the whole, George Friedman was right to stress

> the continuity between the Bush and Obama administrations in regard to foreign policy . . . Dialogue does offer certain possibilities . . . What can't be achieved is a fundamental transformation of the geopolitical realities of the world. No matter how Obama campaigned, it is clear he knows that. Apart from his preoccupation with economic matters, Obama understands that foreign policy is governed by impersonal forces and is not amenable to rhetoric, although rhetoric might make things somewhat easier. No nation gives up its fundamental interests because someone is willing to talk.[55]

The implication of the foregoing analysis is that these 'impersonal forces' leave the US, though weakened by the crisis, still in pole position in the system of states. Nevertheless, the crisis is likely further to destabilize that system and to strengthen the centrifugal forces at work within it. Writing before the implosion of the financial markets, Perry Anderson argued that the US could continue to orchestrate 'a consciously managed Concert of Powers'.[56] But, despite Obama's best efforts, that Concert is likely to be playing more and more out of tune. How great the disharmony will become is hard to predict. The most serious question is, of course, how high the probability is of military conflict developing among the Great Powers, and perhaps most particularly between the US and China. Beijing's steady expansion of its military capabilities is being followed with anxious attention by the Pentagon. The evident transmutation of economic into military power hasn't simply to do merely with the Chinese leadership's long-standing commitment to completing national reunification by incorporating Taiwan into the People's Republic. Analysts have noted the development of what they call a 'string of pearls strategy' aimed at securing a network of naval bases in the Indian Ocean – for example, in Burma, Sri Lanka, and Pakistan.[57] The rationale is apparently to secure China's access to some of the world's biggest trade routes – a perfectly intelligible objective for a state increasingly dependent on maintaining flows of imports and exports, but one that could create tensions with a US whose naval and air power has dominated the Asian littoral since the Pacific War.

But it is important to see that China's emergence as a Great Power is being felt, not only in the Asia-Pacific region, but globally. China's impact as a source of loans, investments and markets is evident throughout the global South. For example, the *New York Times* gloomily reported in April 2009:

> As Washington tries to rebuild its strained relationships in Latin America, China is stepping in vigorously, offering countries across the region large amounts of money while they struggle with sharply slowing economies, a plunge in commodity prices and restricted access to credit.
>
> In recent weeks, China has been negotiating deals to double a development fund in Venezuela to $12bn, lend Ecuador at least $1bn to build a hydroelectric plant, provide Argentina with access to more than $10bn in Chinese currency and lend Brazil's national oil company $10bn. The deals

largely focus on China locking in natural resources like oil for years to come. China's trade with Latin America has grown quickly this decade, making it the region's second largest trading partner after the United States. But the size and scope of these loans point to a deeper engagement with Latin America at a time when the Obama administration is starting to address the erosion of Washington's influence in the hemisphere.

'This is how the balance of power shifts quietly during times of crisis,' said David Rothkopf, a former Commerce Department official in the Clinton administration.[58]

None of these developments makes war between the US and China inevitable, or even very probable. The managers of both states are well aware how disastrous such a conflict would be, and they also understand the extent of their mutual dependence. China will remain both militarily inferior to and much poorer than the US for a long time to come. But they illustrate the difficulties the US faces in playing the role of 'honest broker' mapped out for it by Zakaria, the 'indispensable nation' (in Madeleine Albright's vainglorious phrase) the relationship with which each state values more than its relations with all other states. Other connections may pull states strongly away from the US, and not simply those with China. Germany's dependence on Russian energy supplies is, for example, an important factor undermining NATO's ability to act as a cohesive alliance. If the state system is thus becoming progressively more multipolar, then the interactions of states are liable to become more fluid and unpredictable, and hence more dangerous. One of the great boons of the era since the end of the Cold War has been the comparative rarity of interstate wars. But we cannot bet on this good luck continuing to hold.

Conclusion: Regime Change or System Change?

The end of neoliberalism?

As a result of the economic upheavals in the late 2000s, we are likely to see both a stronger state and a more unstable state system. But what will be the larger socio-economic consequences of the shift in the balance of power between the state and the capital? Robert Wade, a consistent and lucid critic of neoliberalism, writing in October 2008, in the very wake of the financial crash, sensed in the air a change in the economic wind presaging a new policy regime:

> Governmental responses to the crisis . . . suggest that we have entered the second leg of Polanyi's 'double movement', the recurrent pattern in capitalism whereby (to oversimplify) a regime of free markets and increasing commodification generates such suffering and displacement as to prompt attempts to impose closer regulation of markets and de-commodification (hence *'embedded* liberalism').The first leg of the current double movement was the long reign of neoliberalism and its globalization consensus. The second as yet has no name, and may turn out to be a period marked more by a lack of agreement than any new consensus.[1]

Wade went on to sketch out some of the features of such a return to a more regulated capitalism:

> The fallout from complex, opaque financial products may persuade many of the benefits of a substantially smaller financial sector relative to the real one, and perhaps of a 'mixed economy' in finance, where some firms would combine public and private purposes – operating more like utilities than profit maximizers.
>
> But more fundamentally, the globalization model itself needs to be rethought. It over-emphasized capital accumulation or the supply side of the economy, to the detriment of the demand side (since the stress on export-led growth implied that demand was unlimited) . . . Developing domestic and regional demand would involve greater efforts towards achieving equality in the distribution of income – and hence a larger role for labour standards, trade unions, the minimum wage and systems of social protection. It would also necessitate strategic management of trade, so as to curb the race-to-the-bottom effects of export-led growth, and foster domestic industry and services that would provide better livelihoods and incomes for the middle and working classes. Controls on cross-border flows of capital, so as to curb speculative surges, would be another key instrument of a demand-led development process, since they would give governments greater autonomy with regard to the exchange rate and in setting interest rates.[2]

Wade's suggestions would not be palatable to the economic establishment. A few days after he finished his piece, the *Financial Times* carried a remarkable editorial, headlined 'Nationalize to Save the Free Market', in praise of the British government's part-nationalization of the banks:

> Gordon Brown came to save capitalism, not to bury it . . . He now has a growing throng of imitators across the world but they too must act as soon as possible, and in concert, to shore up their ailing financial sectors. These leaders are not putting capitalism to the sword in favour of the gentler

rule of the state. They are using the state to defeat the marketplace's most dangerous historic enemy: widespread depression. And they are right to do so.[3]

The implication of this kind of argument was that the state interventions of 2008–9 were emergency measures, necessary to prevent outright collapse, but presaging no structural change in economic relations. Once a new Great Depression had been averted and the banks had been reorganized and recapitalized, the state should withdraw, like the Lone Ranger, its work done. Consistent with this thinking, even the bolder governments have pursued what one might call a combination of macro-Keynesianism and micro-neoliberalism: New Labour in Britain continued to privatize public services, and Barack Obama's administration sought to deal with the problem of toxic financial assets by subsidizing private investors to buy them.

By contrast, Martin Wolf has taken a somewhat more nuanced position: 'The era of financial liberalization has ended. Yet, unlike in the 1930s, no credible alternative to the market economy exists and the habits of international cooperation are deep.'[4] He is prepared to concede:

> We can guess, therefore, that the age of a hegemonic model of the market economy is past. Countries will, as they have always done, adapt the market economy to their own traditions. But they will do so more confidently. As Mao Zedong might have said, 'Let a thousand capitalist flowers bloom.' A world with many capitalisms will be tricky, but fun . . . To paraphrase what people said on the death of kings: 'Capitalism is dead; long live capitalism.'[5]

Though Wade has been a consistent critic of Wolf's earlier defence of neoliberal globalization, there now seems to be less difference in their positions. Both expect a more pluralistic world economy, but both see the relevant set of alternatives as different varieties of capitalism. This can be brought out by considering Wade's suggestion that the present economic and financial crisis is initiating the latest in a series of oscillations between unrestrained and embedded liberalism. As Wade notes, the underlying idea comes from Karl Polanyi's argument in his classic *The Great Transformation* (1944) that the market economy postulated by classical liberalism requires the forcible disembedding of economic relations from their social context, a move that proves in the long run unsustainable, provoking a reaction back to 'social protection'. John Ruggie draws on Polanyi to claim that at, the end of the Second World War, Western policymakers instituted 'the embedded liberalism compromise: unlike the economic nationalism of the thirties, it would be multilateral in character; unlike the liberalism of the gold standard and free trade, its multilateralism would be predicated upon domestic interventionism'.[6] Neoliberalism, then, represented a reversion back to classical liberalism's attempt to disembed market exchanges from wider social relations that, in a further swing of the pendulum, is now generating a reaction in favour of embedded liberalism.

But what would this reaction involve? It's widely expected that the relative size of finance will shrink in the major economies – in line with Churchill's wish in 1925 to 'see Finance less proud and Industry more content'. But this is less a policy objective that a consequence of the collapse of a sector whose hypertrophy was a symptom of the speculative bubbles it had stimulated: in 2002, finance accounted for 41 per cent of US domestic corporate sector profits.[7] Calls for greater regulation of finance are widespread. France and Germany, in opposing American fiscal expansion, have indeed focused on the need for greater international regulation, targeting tax havens and hedge funds. The Obama administration has proposed much greater regulation of the derivatives market, particularly by encouraging dealers to use exchanges rather than engage in over-the-counter transactions. But are these simply ad hoc measures, like the Sarbanes–Oxley Act 2002 passed by Congress in reaction to the scandals of the dotcom boom, or is a more coherent economic logic likely to emerge? Consider Ruggie's account of postwar embedded liberalism as a synthesis of multilateralism and 'domestic interventionism'. Crucially this combined liberalization at the *international* level with greater state involvement in the economy at the *national* level (expansion of the public sector and of welfare provision and a much more uneven move towards Keynesian demand management). This balance was feasible partly thanks to robust postwar growth rates and partly because under the Bretton Woods agreements states retained (as indeed they still formally do) and exercised the power to regulate capital movements.

The key agency therefore in embedding the market economy in broader socio-political relations was the nation-state. One difficulty today lies in the much higher level of transnational economic integration than prevailed in the postwar era. It was, indeed, the growth in this integration (encouraged notably by the US and Britain) that led states to give up the attempt to control capital flows. One of Wade's main proposals is the restoration of capital controls. The implication is that, once again, the nation-state will be the main agent regulating markets. He tacitly acknowledges the inadequacy of such a solution: 'The recent strengthening of regional integration processes, meanwhile, should direct attention away from global stan dards and arrangements which, because of their maximal scope, are necessarily coarse-grained at best.'[8] There are two difficulties with a reliance on regional integration as an alternative to neoliberal globalization. The first is that many of the most important economic relationships are trans-regional. Asia's main export markets remain the US and Europe. Germany rebuilt its position as number one exporter crucially by supplying complex goods to China. Such economic revival as sub-Saharan Africa and Latin America enjoyed during the boom of the mid-2000s depended especially on China's role in bidding up the price of raw materials. Secondly, as we saw in Chapter 2, states continue to have strongly divergent interests. The EU, widely held up as the model of regional integration for others to follow, has proved itself lamentably ineffective in achieving a coordinated response to the crisis.

Another way of making the same point would be to say that the Great Depression of the 1930s led to much greater economic reliance on the nation-state, initially with cata-strophic consequences (the Second World War), but after 1945 most importantly in the form of the embedded liberal compromise (though outside the West, different versions of a more autarkic state capitalism enjoyed con-siderable economic success). The 'Great Recession' of the 2000s has also led to a turn towards the nation-state, at a time when greater transnational economic integration requires coordinated responses that the state system is unable to provide. Whereas in the mid-twentieth century the nation-state could act as the main regulator of the market, today's globalized markets need international regulation. Moreover, the reason why the existing system of states is unable to play the required role isn't a contin-gent one. The inherently uneven development of capital-ism, which generates concentrated nodes of economic power, promotes tight connections between particular states and capitals. The resulting nexuses of economic and political power constantly tend to pull in diverging directions.[9]

Hence the inability of the G20 summits in November 2008 and April 2009, despite the profound crisis with which they were confronted, to do more than paper over the differences between the leading actors. This doesn't mean, of course, that no coordination among states is pos-sible. On the contrary, one of the key features of the US hegemony has been the institutionalized cooperation of the advanced capitalist states under American leadership. But these arrangements, though they have lasted because they benefitted all the participants, have had the function precisely of helping to secure US hegemony. They are therefore under serious pressure both because of signifi-cant conflicts within the Western bloc (perhaps most importantly those between the US and Germany over both economic policy and relations with Russia) and because of the rise or revival of powers outside this bloc.

This argument, if correct, depends on the proposition that states are themselves embedded in capitalist economic relations. The most important reason why this is so is that, in order to maintain their own power, state managers have a strong incentive to pursue policies that promote capital accumulation within their borders: if they fail to do so, they are likely to be punished by the flight of capital, with negative consequences for the exchange-rate and economic growth. Thus their situation in the global capitalist system strongly encourages state managers to promote the interests of capital.[10] So, if we want to consider how to get out of the present crisis and try to avoid future ones, we need to say a lot more about capitalism. Part of the significance of neoliberalism has been to bring out in a particularly stark and unmediated form the logic of capital itself. In other words, what we are confronted with is not merely, as Wade and Wolf agree, the failure of a particular policy regime and the version of capitalism it has promoted. As I have tried to bring out in Chapter 1, the financial excesses that caused disaster in 2007–9 were essentially a displaced form of a much deeper and more long-standing crisis of overaccumulation and profitability. What has happened, in other words, is a crisis of the capitalist system itself.

Hyman Minsky, from his own post-Keynesian perspective, acknowledges that economic and financial instability are inherent in capitalism. The very mechanisms – the central bank acting as lender of last resort and higher state spending – that prevent a recurrence of the Great Depression encourage the financial innovation that, in boom conditions, leads to bubbles and crises:

> Every time the Federal Reserve protects a financial instrument it legitimizes the use of this instrument to finance activity. This means that not only does Federal Reserve action abort an incipient crisis, but it sets the stage for a resumption in the process of increasing indebtedness – and

makes possible the introduction of new instruments. In effect, the Federal Reserve prepares the way for the restoration of the type of financing that is a necessary, but not a sufficient condition, for an investment boom that is brought to a halt by a financial crisis.

The deficits of Big Government are the sufficient condition. By sustaining aggregate demand, they sustain corporate profits and feed secure assets into portfolios. These effects of Big Government mean that an investment boom will occur quite soon after a recession; and the investment boom generates the demand for finance that leads to another bout of inflation and crisis.[11]

If this analysis is correct, then the very measures that states have taken in response to the financial crash – rescuing the banks and increasing spending and borrowing – will simply encourage yet another speculative boom followed by yet another crisis. There are three possible responses to this. The first is resigned acceptance that this is the way of the world, which seems to have been Minsky's view. The second is the hard-line neoliberal response of letting the banks fail, which embraces catastrophe in the Utopian belief that this will somehow purge capitalism of its impurities. The third is to seek, not a better capitalism, but an alternative to capitalism. This is a tall order. Wolf is right that, unlike the 1930s, no apparent alternatives (however much they may have been idealizations of very different realities) are available. Today at most we see Hugo Chávez's improvised and increasingly embattled experiment in 'twenty-first-century socialism' in Venezuela. This is a symptom of a powerful upsurge of an anti-neoliberal and anti-imperialist left in Latin America – an enormously important political phenomenon rather than a coherent alternative to capitalism itself.[12]

State, market and planning

Nevertheless, the new left governments in Latin America did anticipate the advanced states' response to the economic crisis by extending the role of the state. For example, on 1 May 2006 Evo Morales, newly elected president of Bolivia, sent the army in to seize oil and gas installations to enforce his decree resuming state control of the hydrocarbon industry. Nationalization of the industry was the main demand of the mass insurrection of May–June 2005 that drove from office right-wing president Carlos Mesa. But the movement for another globalization that emerged to contest neoliberalism at the end of the 1990s has often seemed reluctant to see an expansion in the state's economic power. Behind the suspicion of nationalization lies the memory of the bureaucratic state ownership introduced by Stalinism in the East and social democracy in the West. But more immediately influential is the ideology of autonomism, summed up by the title of John Holloway's famous book *Change the World without Taking Power*. In other words, we should forget about the state and try to develop localized alternatives to neoliberalism.[13]

Holloway's approach is hopeless as a general political strategy.[14] It's equally hopeless when confronting the issue at hand. The Bolivian people wanted to reverse the privatization of hydrocarbons. This posed the question of what happens to the hydrocarbon industry when it is taken away from foreign multinationals such as (in this case) Repsol and Petrobras. Inevitably this raised the further question of ownership. In the first instance, there seems no alternative to nationalization (if anything, Morales could be criticized for restoring state control on a basis that fell short of 100 per cent state ownership).[15]

The state is a national organization with both the coercive power and political legitimacy required to carry through something as ambitious as the takeover of the hydrocarbon industry. Moreover, that legitimacy depends critically on the state being able to present itself as responsive to popular demands. This makes it amenable to pressure from below – from mass movements such as that in Bolivia. Morales himself when he was merely leader of the opposition Movement towards Socialism actually opposed the demand to nationalize the hydrocarbon industry. The measure was forced on him by the movement that brought him to office.

None of this means that the contemporary anti-capitalist left should repeat the old mistake of traditional social democracy and identify the existing state as the main agency of progressive social change. As I have already suggested, it is a capitalist state that may respond to mass pressure, but that nevertheless will seek to maintain the domination of capital. To that end it is organized in a bureaucratic and hierarchical manner that seeks above all to exclude popular participation, initiative and control. It was for this reason that Marx argued that any successful revolution against capital has to destroy this state and replace it with a different form of power based on institutions of rank-and-file democracy through which working people can govern themselves.[16]

So nationalization on its own isn't enough. This doesn't alter the significance of what happened in Bolivia: after decades when public assets were sold off for private profit, popular revolt against neoliberalism actually forced one government to take something back – and not just any old something, as is made clear by the howls of agony sent out by the global political and business establishment when the Morales government seized the oil and gas industry. This experience confirms the following remarks by Antoine Artous: 'I don't see how we can unleash a dynamic of social transformation without, if not straightaway over-throwing, at least profoundly modifying certain property relations.' Artous goes on to point out that nationalization isn't enough: 'The whole concept of social appropriation can't be reduced to the simple legal transfer of titles of property. It presupposes a wholesale challenge to the capitalist division of labour (the hierarchical organization of production) and its replacement by cooperative forms of production.'[17]

Indeed, really to break with the logic of capital, any extension of the boundaries of state ownership would have to involve the introduction of forms of democratic self-

management through which the workers of the nationalized industry together with the consumers of their products
could collectively decide on how it should be run for the
common benefit. Seriously addressing this question means
breaking another taboo and talking, not just about state
ownership, but also about planning. From the 1930s
onwards planning became identified with the bureaucratic
command economies of the Soviet Union and its client
states. As long as these flourished, then planning enjoyed
great prestige and was, for example, copied by postcolo-
nial states such as India and Egypt. The decline and fall of
the USSR totally discredited planning and helped to legitimize neoliberalism. The reigning economic orthodoxy sys-
tematically conceals the extent to which some of the most
successful economies in the contemporary world – for
example, China and South Korea – have depended on state
intervention.

The reaction against planning has meant that even those
seeking to develop alternatives to capitalism as such have
seen some kind of market economy as inescapable. This is
most obviously true of the market socialism advocated, for
example, by the philosopher David Miller and the economist John Roemer. Here collectively owned cooperatives
compete to sell their products on the market. Even the
Marxist philosopher Tony Smith argues that it would be
possible to democratize the market.[18]

The fundamental problem with this kind of strategy is
that it is a necessary feature of a market economy that it
is based on competition. In a market economy the allocation of resources is the unintended outcome of competition
between the capitals that jointly but not collectively control
the economy. In other words, each firm's share of resources
depends on how successful it is in selling its goods or services on the market. There is no collective decision by
society at large about how resources are allocated. And if
a capital fails to compete, then it loses its share of resources
– it goes bankrupt. So the individual units of a market
economy tend to be under systematic pressure to cut their

costs of production and thereby reduce the prices of their products in order to stay competitive. It is the resulting process of competitive accumulation that underlies the tendency towards profound crises such as the present one.

Now this set up can't be organized democratically. By definition, it can't be organized democratically at the level of the economy as a whole, because there are no collective decisions about the allocation of resources, democratic or otherwise. But it's also very hard to sustain democratic organization within the individual firm as well. Michael Albert explains this very well. Let's imagine, he suggests, a worker-controlled enterprise that is organized on a democratic and egalitarian basis but that is failing to sell its products. What will the workers do?

> In this context, assuming that they reject bankruptcy, they have two broad choices: They can opt to reduce their own wages, worsen their own work conditions, and speed up their own levels of work, which is a very alienating approach that they are not very emotionally or psychologically equipped to undertake. Or, they can hire managers to carry out these cost-cutting and output enlarging policies while insulating the managers from feeling the policies' adverse effects by giving the managers better conditions, higher wages, etc. In practice, very predictably, the latter is what occurs . . . markets therefore have a built-in pressure to organize a workforce into two groups: a large majority that obeys and a small minority that makes decisions, with the latter enjoying greater income, power, and protection from the adverse effects of the cost-cutting decisions they will impose on others.[19]

The logic of a market economy therefore tends to undermine and eventually to overwhelm any islands of democracy and equality that may emerge within it. This means that socialists such as Roemer and Smith who believe that it is possible to democratize the market tend to face a dilemma of their own. Either they impose restrictions on the functioning of the market to prevent it from eroding democracy, in which case any economy based on the principles they propose is likely to break down because they prevent the logic of competition from operating properly, or, if they allow this logic to operate, it will destroy the socialist ideals they are trying to realize and generate the systemic instability that this book has sought to diagnose.

There are other strong reasons to press for a break with the logic of competitive accumulation. The scientific evidence that the emission of greenhouse gases – most notably CO_2 – caused by human activity is generating profound and irreversible processes of climate change is now beyond dispute. It is also very widely agreed that preventing these processes reaching a disastrous scale requires the rapid adoption and implementation of drastic targets for cutting CO^2 emissions. But while the targets, particularly since the eclipse of the Bush gang, have become more ambitious, the actual emissions have continued to rise. The most plausible explanation appeals to the logic of competition.

The problem is, yet again, one of collective action. Evidently it is in everyone's interest to avoid drastic climate change. But no individual capital or state is willing to shoulder the additional costs involved in moving to a low-carbon economy. In international negotiations, the leading states play a game of pass-the-parcel – the US demanding that India and China adopt tough targets, the latter asking why they should bear the burden of two centuries of industrialization mainly in the North. The EU, despite its pretensions to be a master of 'soft power' that has transcended bad old nationalism, is particularly ineffectual. Germany has vocally and largely successfully defended its car firms against what they regarded as excessively tough targets. And the economic crisis has provided many governments with a perfect excuse to go slow in reducing reliance on fossil fuels. The logic of competitive accumulation here threatens the future of the human species.[20]

The implication is that any sustainable alternative to capitalism has to be based, not on the market, but on democratic planning. In a democratically planned economy the allocation of resources would be the outcome of a democratic political process that would set overall priorities for the economy. There are some models of how this could work. One is Albert's Parecon, or participatory economics. This involves an economy of workers' and consumers' councils in which individuals and enterprises submit proposals for their share of society's resources and a process of gradual adjustments (Albert calls them 'iterations') takes place while technical experts come up with a plan that would give everyone as much as possible of what they want.

The main weakness of this model is that it mimics a bit too closely the workings of a market economy, in which claims on resources are driven by individual demands. Albert is an anarchist, and his commitment to decentralization here goes too far. The allocation of society's resources isn't a neutral technical issue. It's a political question that requires some sort of collective and democratic decision-making process to choose between what would often be competing views of the priorities of the society in question. From this perspective, Pat Devine offers a superior model of what he calls negotiated coordination. Here the allocation of resources is largely the outcome of discussion between producers, consumers and other affected groups, but within the framework of overall decisions about economic priorities made democratically at the national and international level.[21]

Plainly there is much more to be said – and, above all, to be done – about democratic planning. All the same, the importance of the kind of work being done by Albert, Devine and others is that they begin to break down the prejudice against planning and to sketch out how an economy that rejected the market could manage to be both democratic and efficient. But any break with capitalism couldn't take the form of an instantaneous leap into a fully planned economy. Marx long ago argued in the 'Critique of the Gotha Programme' that a new workers' state would inherit a society deeply marked by capitalism. Initially, it would have to make compromises with the old order, and gradually move towards a society governed by the communist principle 'From each according to his ability, to each according to his needs!'[22]

Similarly today a government breaking with capitalism would need to make a decisive shift towards an economy in which priorities were decided democratically rather than left to the anarchy of competition. This would involve critically taking control of the financial markets, nationalizing under workers' control key sectors of the economy, and extending social provision on the basis of a progressive tax system that redistributed wealth and income from rich to poor. These measures, radical though they are, would still leave in place many aspects of a market economy. Large sectors would remain in private hands. Continuous pressure and the introduction of new measures would be necessary to move the economy as a whole towards the principles of democratic planning. One key step would be to weaken the power of the capitalist labour market, which today rules our lives.

In my view, the best way to do this would be to introduce universal direct income. In other words, every resident of the country would receive, as of right, an income that met their basic needs at a relatively low but nevertheless decent level. This would serve two goals. First, it would ensure a basic level of welfare for everyone much more efficiently than existing systems of social provision. (People with greater needs because they had children or were disabled or whatever would receive a higher basic income.) Secondly, having a guaranteed basic income would greatly reduce the pressure on individuals to accept whatever job was on offer on the labour market. One of the main presuppositions of capitalism – that workers have no acceptable alternative to wage labour – would be removed. The balance of power between labour and capital would shift towards the workers, irrespective of the nature of their employer.[23]

More broadly, the question of power is crucial. One obvious challenge to the kind of vision of change I have just sketched out is how to ensure that the direction of change would be towards a democratically planned economy rather than back to market capitalism or maybe to the kind of state capitalism that ended up dominating the Soviet Union. The only guarantee that counts is that levers of political power are in the hands of the workers and the poor themselves. As long as the state takes the form that it does today, of a bureaucratically organized, hierarchical set of apparatuses whose managers' interests are bound up with those of capital, any improvement in society can only be temporary and fragile. This is why the strategy of ignoring the state advocated by Holloway is so badly mistaken. If we are to move towards a democratically planned economy, then the existing state has to be confronted and broken.

This task can only be achieved through the development of a different kind of power, one based on the self-organization of workers and other poor people that develops out of their struggles against capital. The great revolutionary movements of the twentieth century offered some glimpses of this power – from the workers' and soldiers' councils of the Russian Revolution of October 1917 to the workers' *shoras* during the Iranian Revolution of 1978–9. The self-organization displayed by the Bolivian popular movement during the insurrections of October 2003 and May–June 2005 showed that the contemporary movements against neoliberalism can generate this kind of power as well.[24]

A democratically planned economy would be the core of a self-managing society, one in which directly elected workplace and neighbourhood councils took responsibility for their own affairs and linked together to make decisions for society at large. The key insight that Marx had during the Paris Commune of 1871 was that these forms of organization would develop *before* the new society was created, in the process of fighting the old society. The same methods of self-organization that would be the basis of a self-managing society are needed by the exploited and oppressed to resist and, ultimately, to overthrow capital itself.

The overthrow of capital is itself a process. The dilemma that Albert imagines confronting a workers' cooperative in a market economy would face any society that was beginning to introduce the principles of democratic planning in a world still ruled by capitalism. It was responsible for the corruption and eventual destruction of the Russian Revolution of October 1917. Any breakthrough in one part of the world could only survive by spreading and progressively overturning the logic of capital on a global scale. The globalization of capital has produced a globalization of resistance. Struggles in different parts of the world contaminate each other. Chiapas and Seattle had global reverberations. The two European countries with the most advanced and combative social movements, France and Greece, have exerted a degree of mutual influence on one another. The movements in Latin America have become a beacon to all those fighting neoliberalism.

We are still a very long way from overturning capitalism even in one country. Indeed, the more one seeks to elaborate on the shape of an alternative to capitalism the more one is overawed by the immensity of the task. The biggest immediate obstacle that confronts anyone seeking to address it is the chronic political weakness of the radical anticapitalist left on a global scale. Nevertheless, the present crisis has torn a huge hole in neoliberalism both as an ideology and as a mode of organizing capitalism. The market no longer seems like a second nature unamenable to change or control. Those who are prepared to seize this moment boldly can help to ensure that the boundaries of the possible really are widened, allowing the billions of victims of capitalism finally to escape.

Notes

Introduction: How the World Changed in 2008

1 Alain Badiou has written the most important contemporary philosophical discussion of the event: see, in particular, *L'Etre et l'évenement* (Paris, 1988) and *Logiques des mondes* (Paris, 2006).

2 F. Fukuyama, *The End of History and the Last Man* (New York, 1992). The spirit of this age is exemplified by the ineffable Bernard Kouchner, currently French Foreign Minister, skewered by Pierre Péan in his devastating and hilarious portrait *Le Monde selon K.* (Paris, 2009).

3 *The National Security Strategy of the United States of America*, September 2002, www.georgewbush-whitehouse. archives.gov, p. iv.

4 See the reconstruction of events in 'Countdown in the Caucasus', *Financial Times*, 26 August 2008.

5 G. Friedman, 'The Medvedev Doctrine and American Strategy', 2 September 2008, www.stratfor.com.

6 Ibid.

7 Especially G. Arrighi, *Adam Smith in Beijing* (London, 2007), ch. 7.

8 Quoted in Q. Peel, 'Why Russia Threw Down the Gauntlet to Obama', *Financial Times*, 7 February 2009.

9 B. Benoit and J. Thornhill, 'Sarkozy Says Era of Laissez Faire is Finished', *Financial Times*, 26 September 2008.

10 R. C. Altman, 'The Great Crash, 2008: A Geopolitical Setback for the West', *Foreign Affairs*, 88:1 (January/February 2009), p. 2.

11 L. Elliott, 'The Overweening Pride that Came Before Calamitous Fall', *Guardian*, 22 April 2009.

12 IMF, *World Economic Outlook*, October 2007, www.imf.org, p. 87.

13 IMF, *World Economic Outlook*, April 2009, www.imf.org, p. 109.

14 A. J. P. Taylor, *English History 1914–1945* (Harmondsworth, 1970), p. 373.

15 The role played by nation-states in breaking up the liberal world economy during the Great Depression is the main theme of H. James, *The End of Globalization* (Cambridge MA, 2001).

16 N. Ferguson, 'Memo to Market Dinosaurs', *Financial Times*, 13 December 2007.

17 T. Barber and E. Luce, 'EU Leader Condemns US "Road to Hell"', *Financial Times*, 26 March 2009.

18 'Peer Steinbrück on the Global Economic Crisis', *Newsweek*, 15 December 2008.

19 See Peter Clarke's excellent study, *The Keynesian Revolution in the Making, 1924–1936* (Oxford, 1988).

20 G. D. H. Cole, *Practical Economics* (Harmondsworth, 1937), pp. 21, 249.

21 See, for example, D. Harvey, *A Short History of Neoliberalism* (Oxford, 2005). Neoliberalism is often conceptualized, particularly by its left-wing critics, as far more homogenous and coherent than it actually is: for a powerful corrective to such thinking see C. Harman, 'Theorizing Neoliberalism', *International Socialism*, 2.117 (2008). Ben Fine puts it very well: 'neoliberalism comprises a complex, generally inconsistent but related, articulation across a portfolio of ideology, scholarship, policy in practice and representation of reality itself', 'Financialization, Neoliberalism, and the Crisis', forthcoming in *Historical Materialism*. Here I am primarily interested in it as an economic policy regime: see below and Chapter 1.

22 For this anecdote, and the general embarrassment of main-stream economics, see C. Giles, 'The Economic Forecasters' Failing Vision', *Financial Times*, 16 December 2008.

23 N. N. Taleb, 'The Pseudo-Science Hurting Markets', *Financial Times*, 23 October 2007. Two interesting critiques from within the economic profession are D. Colander et al., 'The Financial Crisis and the Systemic Failure of Academic Economics', *Kiel Working Papers*, no. 1489, February 2009, www.ifw-members.ifw-kiel.de, and T. Lawson, 'The Current Economic Crisis: Its Nature and the Course of Academic Economics', *Cambridge Journal of Economics*, 33 (2009). A searching examination of mainstream economics and its influence on other social sciences will be found in the work of Ben Fine and Dimitris Milonakis, notably *From Political Economy to Economics* (London, 2009), and *From Economics Imperialism to Freakonomics* (London, 2009).

24 Transcript, 'The Financial Crisis and the Role of Federal Regulators', 23 October 2008, House of Representatives, Committee on Oversight and Government Reform, www.oversight.house.gov.

25 A. Smith, *An Inquiry into the Nature and Causes of the Wealth of Nations* (2 vols., Oxford, 1976) IV.ii, I, p. 456.

26 M. Skapinker, 'The Market No Longer Has All the Answers', *Financial Times*, 25 March 2008.

27 'The Consequence of Bad Economics', *Financial Times*, 9 March 2009.

28 M. Wolf, *Why Globalization Works* (Yale, 2004), p. 266.

29 M. Wolf, *Fixing Global Finance* (Yale, 2009). See my review, 'An Apologist with Insights', *International Socialism*, 2.122 (2009).

30 M. Wolf, 'Keynes Offers Us to the Best Way to Think about the Crisis', *Financial Times*, 24 December 2008. Compare his much more even-handed response to Friedman's death: 'Keynes v. Friedman: Both Can Claim Victory', ibid., 21 November 2006.

31 M. Wolf, 'Why the G20 Must Focus on Sustaining Demand', *Financial Times*, 10 March 2009.

32 S. Brittan, 'Keynes, Thou Should'st Be Living . . .', *Financial Times*, 9 October 2008, and 'Why the Brown Critics Are Wrong', ibid., 20 November 2008.

33 See, for example, M. H. Best and W. E. Connolly, *The Politicized Economy* (2nd edn; Lexington MA, 1982).

34 F. A. von Hayek, *New Studies in the Philosophy, Politics, Economics and the History of Ideas* (London, 1978), p. 208. Hayek's position is not the same as Friedman's. He calls monetarism 'the exposition of a somewhat mechanical form of the quantity theory of money', and argues, against Friedman, a point relevant in present conditions, that, 'in order to ensure the convertibility of all kinds of near-money into real money, which is necessary if we are to avoid severe liquidity crises or panics, the monetary authorities must be given some discretion', ibid., pp. 215, 208. See the lucid presentation of the debate provoked by Friedman in S. Brittan, *How to End the 'Monetarist' Controversy* (London, 1982).

35 A. Callinicos, *Against the Third Way* (Cambridge, 2001).

36 W. Benjamin, *Illuminations* (ed. H. Arendt; London, 1970), p. 255.

37 'Turning Their Backs on the World', *The Economist*, 19 February 2009. Compare W. Bello, *Deglobalization* (London, 2002).

38 J. Politi and D. Dombey, 'Republican Anger at "Financial Socialism"', *Financial Times*, 24 September 2008.

39 S. Žižek, 'Use Your Illusions', *London Review of Books*, 14 November 2008. Žižek explores the ideological dimensions of the crisis in *First as Tragedy, Then as Farce* (London, 2009), ch. 1.

40 Wolf, *Why Globalization Works*, p. xi.

41 See especially D. Harvey, *The New Imperialism* (Oxford, 2003), and A. Callinicos, *Imperialism and Global Political Economy* (Cambridge, 2009).

42 Presentations of Marx's economic thought will be found in A. Callinicos, *The Revolutionary Ideas of Karl Marx* (London, 1983); B. Fine and A. Saad-Filho, *Marx's Capital* (London, 2004); and J. Choonara, *Unravelling Capitalism* (London, 2009). Chris Harman's *Zombie Capitalism: Global Crisis and the History of Capitalism* (London, 2009) puts the present crisis in the context of the theory and history of capitalism.

1 Finance Humbled

1 W. S. Churchill, letter to Otto Nietmeyer, 22 February 1925, quoted in D. E. Moggridge, *Maynard Keynes: An Economist's Biography* (London, 1995), p. 428. On the background, see ibid., ch. 17; R. Skidelsky, *John Maynard Keynes* (3 vols., London, 1983, 1992 and 2000), II, ch. 6; R. Jenkins, *Churchill* (London, 2001), pp. 398–402; and L. Ahamad, *Lords of Finance* (London, 2009), ch. 12.

2 R. Chernow, *The House of Morgan* (New York, 1990), chs. 14 and 18.

3 S. Johnson, 'The Silent Coup', *Atlantic Monthly*, May 2009.

4 Ibid. See also the ferocious assault on Goldman Sachs in M. Taibbi, 'The Great American Bubble Machine', *Rolling Stone*, July 2009.

5 P. Gowan, 'Crisis in the Heartland', *New Left Review*, II/55 (2009). A mainstream analysis of the financial crisis that also overlaps with more radical diagnoses is provided by Lord Turner, chair of the UK Financial Services Authority: *The Turner Review: A Regulatory Response to the Global Banking Crisis*, March 2009, www.fsa.gov.uk.

6 G. Dymski, 'Racial Exclusion and the Political Economy of the Subprime Crisis', *Historical Materialism*, 17.2 (2009) (quotations from pp. 162, 164).

7 A Greenspan, *The Age of Turbulence* (London, 2007), p. 233.

8 See also the discussion in C. Harman, *Zombie Capitalism: Global Crisis and the Relevance of Marx* (London, 2009), ch. 11.

9 G. Duménil and D. Lévy, *Capital Resurgent* (Cambridge MA, 2004), p. 69.

10 R. Hilferding, *Finance Capital* (London, 1981).

11 Chernow, *The House of Morgan*, p. 486. For much more extensive discussion of Hilferding, see A. Callinicos, *Imperialism and Global Political Economy* (Cambridge, 2009), esp. ch. 1; and C. Lapavitsas, 'Financialized Capitalism: Crisis and Financial Expropriation', *Historical Materialism*, 17.2 (2009), pp. 143–6.

12 E.g., J. Grahl, 'Globalized Finance', *New Left Review*, II/8 (2001), pp. 25–7.

13 F. Chesnais, *La Mondialisation du capital* (rev. edn; Paris, 1997), p. 243; see generally ibid., ch. 10.

14 C. Lapavitsas, 'Financialized Capitalism: Direct Exploitation and Periodic Bubbles', May 2008, http://www.soas.ac.uk/economics/events/crisis/43939.pdf, p. 34.

15 *The Turner Review*, p. 21.

16 Gowan, 'Crisis in the Heartland', p. 10.

17 G. Tett and P. J. Davies, 'Out of the Shadows: How Banking's Secret System Broke Down', *Financial Times*, 17 December 2007.

18 B. Gross, 'Beware Our Shadow Banking System', 28 November 2007, www.money.cnn.com.

19 'Speech by Dr Alan Greenspan on World Finance and Risk Management at Lancaster House', 25 September 2002, www.hm-treasury.gov.uk.

20 International Monetary Fund, *Global Financial Stability Report*, April 2006, www.imf.org, p. 51.

21 G. Tett, *Fool's Gold: How Unrestrained Greed Corrupted a Dream, Shattered Global Markets and Unleashed a Catastrophe* (London, 2009), pp. 160, 240.

22 Marcel Koonings argues that a relatively high level of participation in the financial system by small farmers and workers, as both savers and borrowers, has been a distinctive feature of American capitalism from the early years of the US onwards: 'American Finance and Empire in Historical Perspective', in L. Panitch and M. Koonings, eds, *American Empire and the Political Economy of Global Finance* (Basingstoke, 2008).

23 See K. Marx, *Capital*, II (Harmondsworth, 1978), ch. 2.

24 M. Itoh and C. Lapavitsas, *Political Economy of Money and Finance* (London, 1999), p. 61. See more generally K. Marx, *Capital*, III (Harmondsworth, 1981), Part 5.

25 Itoh and Lapavitsas, *Political Economy of Money and Finance*, p. 70.

26 Though my discussion of financialization is heavily indebted to Lapavitsas's work, I part company with him when he argues that the profits banks make by lending to working-class households constitutes 'direct exploitation' that bypasses the extraction of surplus-value in production. As he notes, 'finance directed at personal revenue is advanced to cover basic needs of workers and others – housing,

pensions, consumption, and so on', 'Financialized Capitalism: Direct Exploitation and Periodic Bubbles', p. 15. (In the later version of this paper published in *Historical Materialism*, Lapavitsas has retreated to the more neutral expression 'financial appropriation'.) From the perspective of Marxist value theory, workers are borrowing to help cover the costs of reproduction of their labour-power. These are costs that fall on capital, in the sense that they must be met before any surplus-value can be appropriated. To the extent that through helping to finance these costs banking capitalists derive a profit in the form of interest, fees, etc., this profit should be understood as a redistribution of surplus-value from industrial and commercial capitalists. A much deeper and more complex critical engagement with Lapavitsas will be found in B. Fine, 'Financialization, Neoliberalism and the Crisis', forthcoming in *Historical Materialism*.

27 G. Soros, 'The Game Changer', *Financial Times*, 28 January 2009.

28 D. Bryan and M. Rafferty, *Capitalism with Derivatives* (Basingstoke, 2006), pp. 52, 131.

29 Ibid., pp. 13, 132, 133, 134. Suggestive though Bryan and Rafferty's analysis is, I dissent from their conclusion that '[d]erivatives, their anchoring function for global finance, play the role of a commodity money' once performed by gold: ibid., p. 132. For example, the CDOs and CDSs that became unmarketable as a result of the crisis lack a basic quality of money, namely liquidity.

30 M. Mackenzie, 'Derivatives Contracts Volume Tumble', *Financial Times*, 19 May 2009.

31 Bryan and Rafferty, *Capitalism with Derivatives*, p. 59.

32 Quoted in R. J. Shiller, *Irrational Exuberance* (Princeton, 2001), p. 172

33 M. Wolf, *Fixing Global Finance* (New Haven, 2009), p. 31.

34 Hence the ineptitude of a study of the last time a financial crash in the US precipitated a severe slump, in 1907, that warned, on the eve of the credit crunch, that 'adverse leadership' from anti-market politicians such as Hugo Chávez, Vladimir Putin, and Franz Münterfering of the German Social Democratic Party could precipitate another crash:

R. F. Bruner and S. D. Carr, *The Panic of 1907* (Hoboken NJ, 2007), p. 175. The 'adverse leadership' proved to come from such paladins of the free market as George Bush, Alan Greenspan and Hank Paulson.

35 J. Schumpeter, *A History of Economic Analysis* (New York, 1954), p. 277. See Itoh and Lapavitas, *Political Economy of Money and Banking*, ch. 1, on classical approaches.

36 Quoted in H. Minsky, *Stabilizing an Unstable Economy* (New York, 2008), p. 129.

37 Ibid., pp. 4, 5.

38 J. M. Keynes, letter to H. D. Henderson, 28 May 1936, in *The Collected Writings of John Maynard Keynes*, XXIX (ed. D. Moggridge; London, 1979), p. 222.

39 J. M. Keynes, *The General Theory of Employment, Interest and Money* (London, 1970), p. 293. Two interesting discussions of Keynes and Minsky in relation to the present crisis, which stress the differences between them and between both and 'Keynesian' policies are E. Tymoigne, 'Minsky and Economic Policy: "Keynesianism" All Over Again?', October 2008, www.levy.org, and A. Leijonhufvud, 'Out of the Corridor: Keynes and the Crisis', *Cambridge Journal of Economics*, 33 (2009).

40 F. H. Knight, *Risk, Uncertainty, and Profit* (Boston, 1921), esp. ch. VII, available at www.econlib.org/library/Knight/knRUP.html.

41 G. Tett and A. Gangahar, 'Limitations of Computer Models', *Financial Times*, 14 August 2007. The failure of financial-market actors to understand probability is one of the main themes of Nassim Nicholas Taleb's writing: for example, *Fooled by Randomness* (2nd edn; London, 2007).

42 Minsky, *Stabilizing an Unstable Economy*, p. 207.

43 Ibid., pp. 134, 232. Charles Ponzi was the author of a 1920 financial scam reliant on a continuous stream of new investors whose contributions provide the returns of earlier investors. Bernard Madoff was sentenced in 2009 to 150 years in gaol for ripping $65bn off his clients in a similar way. Minsky, however, is using the term neutrally.

44 Minsky, *Stabilizing an Unstable Economy*, pp. 233, 237–8.

45 Ibid., pp. 264, 280.

46 Ibid., pp. 48–9.

47 Ibid., pp. 370, 194.
48 Keynes, *The General Theory of Employment, Interest and Money*, p. 378.
49 Minsky, *Stabilizing an Unstable Economy*, p. 364.
50 F. A. von Hayek, *Prices and Production* (rev. edn; London, 1935), p. 126. He also, like Marx and Keynes, argues that Say's Law, that supply and demand are necessarily identical, ceases to hold 'as soon as money becomes the intermediary of the exchange transactions', ibid., p. 130.
51 Ibid., p. 55, 57, 57–8.
52 Ibid., p. 55,
53 Ibid., pp. 89–90, 98, 99.
54 J. Strachey, *The Theory of Capitalist Crisis* (London, 1935), p. 241. See ibid., chs. IV and V for a detailed discussion of *Prices and Production*, which Strachey describes as 'the most interesting capitalist attempt to describe and account for the trade cycle', ibid., p. 58.
55 Valuable treatments of Marx's theory of crisis will be found in B. Fine and L. Harris, *Rereading Capital* (London, 1979); J. Weeks, *Capital and Exploitation* (Princeton, 1981); D. Harvey, *The Limits to Capital* (Oxford, 1982); C. Harman, *Explaining the Crisis* (London, 1984), and *Zombie Capitalism*; G. Carchedi, *Frontiers of Political Economy* (London, 1991); and S. Clarke, *Marx's Theory of Crisis* (London, 1994).
56 Marx, *Capital*, III, p. 597.
57 Ibid., p. 572.
58 Harvey, *The Limits to Capital*, pp. 191, 326, 285–6. For a brief note of dissent to Harvey's broadening of Marx's first-cut theory, see Callinicos, *Imperialism and Global Political Economy*, pp. 257–8 n. 8.
59 Harvey, *The Limits to Capital*, p. 286.
60 Ibid., p. 251.
61 Ibid., p. 280. See also the discussion of inflation, ibid., pp. 307–15.
62 International Monetary Fund, *World Economic Outlook*, April 2009, www.imf.org, pp. 9, xvii.
63 David McNally's 'From Financial Crisis to World Slump', *Historical Materialism*, 17.2 (2009), offers a stimulating and instructive panoramic overview of the crisis. But it is seriously weakened by a false and essentially polemical

counterposition of what McNally presents as two mistaken approaches to the crisis on the left – on the one hand, those 'who view the financial meltdown as just the latest manifestation of a crisis of profitability that began in the early 1970s, a crisis that has effectively persisted since that time' (pp. 41–2), and, on the other, those 'who see the crisis as essentially caused by an explosion of financial transactions and speculation that followed from deregulation of financial markets over the past quarter-century' (p. 42). McNally contends that the former 'tend to be amazingly static, ignoring the specific dynamics of capitalist restructuring and accumulation in the neoliberal period', positing a permanent crisis lasting nearly forty years and thus denying the recovery of profitability and growth that started in the early 1980s; '[t]he latter . . . suffer from a failure to grasp the deep tendencies at the level of capital accumulation and profitability that drove deregulation and that underpin this crisis' (p. 42). Though I am more sympathetic to the first approach criticized, I must say that McNally is thoroughly unfair to both. Thus Duménil and Lévy, though reducing neoliberalism to the domination of finance, situate their analysis in a broader analysis of the dynamics of capital accumulation and profitability, but argue (mistakenly in my view) that capitalism succeeded in overcoming the structural crisis it suffered in the 1970s and 1980s: see *Capital Resurgent*, Part II. As for the first approach, McNally himself tacitly acknowledges that its best-known exponent, Robert Brenner, integrates into his analysis the capital restructuring and partial recovery of profitability that occurred in the 1980s and 1990s: see especially *The Economics of Global Turbulence* (London, 2006), chs. 12–14. The rhetorical effect of McNally's misrepresentation of the view taken by Brenner and those who think like him is to give greater originality to his own position, namely that 'neoliberal recovery in profit rates and the wave of capitalist expansion it sustained began to run up against powerful limits by the late 1990s' and that, accordingly, while 'the entire period after 1982 cannot be explained in terms of credit creation, the postponement of a general crisis *after* 1997 can' (p. 55), than it actually merits. Much more satisfactory overviews will be found in Brenner and in Harman, *Zombie Capitalism*, Part III.

64 See up-to-date data presented in Brenner, *The Economics of Global Turbulence*, Afterword. For an earlier analysis that also explains what Brenner calls the 'long downturn' as a crisis of profitability, see Harman, *Explaining the Crisis*, pp. 90–102. The original publication of Brenner's analysis, which offers a different explanation for falling profitability from Marx's, as 'The Economics of Global Turbulence', *New Left Review*, I/229 (1998), provoked a considerable debate among Marxist economists: see especially *Historical Materialism* 4 and 5 (1999). My own take on the argument will be found in 'Capitalism, Competition and Profits: A Critique of Robert Brenner's Theory of Crisis', *Historical Materialism*, 4 (1999). For more recent discussion of profitability, see C. Harman, 'The Rate of Profit and the World Today', *International Socialism*, 2.115 (2007), the responses by Jim Kincaid, Harman and Fred Moseley, ibid., 2.119 (2008), A. Kliman, 'Pinning the Blame on the System', ibid., 2.124 (2009), and Harman, 'Not All Marxism is Dogmatism: A Reply to Michel Husson', ibid., 2.125 (2010).

65 McNally, 'From Financial Crisis to World Slump', p. 45.

66 M. Kidron, 'A Permanent Arms Economy', *International Socialism*, 1.28 (1967), available at www.marxists.org, and *Western Capitalism since the War* (Harmondsworth, 1970), and Harman, *Explaining the Crisis*, pp. 75–90 and *Zombie Capitalism*, chs. 4, 5, and 7.

67 C. Dow, *Major Recessions: Britain and the World, 1920–1995* (Oxford, 1995), p. 2.

68 Greenspan, *The Age of Turbulence*, p. 268.

69 See the helpful discussion of the devaluation of capital in Harvey, *The Limits to Capital*, pp. 84–5 and ch. 7.

70 Duménil and Lévy, *Capital Resurgent*, p. 69.

71 Brenner, *The Economics of Global Turbulence*, pp. 196–7.

72 S. Mohun, 'Distributive Shares in the US Economy, 1964–2001', *Cambridge Journal of Economics*, 30 (2006), pp. 357, 358. Mohun's research is significant because, unlike Brenner, he uses the concepts of Marxist value theory to arrive at broadly similar conclusions about the behaviour of the rate of profit. Thus he takes into account the distinc-

tion between productive and unproductive labour (only the former creates value, according to Marxist value theory) and includes in surplus-value the income of supervisory workers, who he characterizes as 'the bearers of the capital relation' (p. 263). This seems like an overstatement, for reasons explored at length in A. Callinicos and C. Harman, *The Changing Working Class* (London, 1987), available at www.isj.org.uk, but it is nevertheless striking that, even on this assumption (which significantly increases the mass of surplus-value), the trend in profitability posited by Brenner holds up.

73 S. Mohun, 'Aggregate Capital Productivity in the US Economy, 1964–2001', forthcoming in *Cambridge Journal of Economics*, advance access at www.cjc.oxfordjournals. org, December 2008.

74 G. Duménil and D. Levy, 'The Profit Rate: Where and How Much Did It Fall? Did It Recover?', *Review of Radical Political Economy*, 34 (2002), p. 439.

75 Mohun, 'Aggregate Capital Productivity in the US Economy, 1964–2001', p. 3. Fred Mosley argues that 'there has been a very substantial and probably almost complete recovery of the rate of profit in the US', but his own figures show the rate of profit, after rising again in the early 2000s, starting to fall before the onset of the subprime crisis in 2007: 'The US Economic Crisis: Causes and Solutions', *Marxism 21*, 6:1 (2009), p. 301, Figure 1, p. 315. Two Goldman Sachs economists claim that 'the global return on physical capital rose through the 2000s', but they rely on the dubious ploy of including capital gains, which of course boosts profitability at the height of the bubble; using what they call the yield on capital (net operating surplus over capital stock) produces results similar to Brenner's for the ten biggest economies: K. Daly and B. Broadbent, 'The Savings Glut, the Return on Capital and the Rise in Risk Aversion', *Goldman Sachs Global Economic Paper*, no. 185, 27 May 2009, www.360.gs.com, p. 2. I am grateful to Joseph Choonara for confirming my conceptual hunch about this and for demonstrating the similarity in results: see 'A Note on Goldman Sachs and the Rate of Profit', *International Socialism*, 2.124 (2009)

76 Harvey, *The Limits to Capital*, p. 195.

77 E. V. Preobrazhensky, *The Decline of Capitalism* (Armonk NY, 1985).

78 Harvey, *The Limits to Capital*, pp. 425, 428; see generally ibid., chs. 11–13.

79 Ibid., p. 428. The contradictions of the spatial expansion of capital are central to Harvey's theory of imperialism: see ibid., pp. 439–45, and *The New Imperialism* (Oxford, 2003).

80 McNally, 'From Financial Crisis to World Slump', pp. 43, 47, 50.

81 R. Brenner, *The Boom and the Bubble* (London, 2002), chs. 4 and 6.

82 For an excellent analysis of this process, see E. Helleiner, *States and the Reemergence of Global Finance* (Ithaca, 1994). According to Misha Glenny, one unintended consequence of financial liberalization was the rapid spread of transnational crime networks: *McMafia: Crime without Frontiers* (London, 2008).

83 Helleiner, *States and the Reemergence of Global Finance*, pp. 112, 113–14.

84 P. Gowan, *The Global Gamble* (London, 1999). See also R. H. Wade, 'The Invisible Hand of the American Empire', *Ethics and International Affairs*, 17 (2003). On devaluation as a tool for restoring US competitiveness (which Gowan and Wade insufficiently stress), see, for example, R. Parboni, *The Dollar and Its Rivals* (London, 1981), and Brenner, *The Boom and the Bubble*, ch. 2.

85 Wolf, *Fixing Global Finance*, p. 76.

86 Ibid., p. 87. In a series of incisive analyses J. Taggart Murphy has traced the origins of this system earlier, to Japan's response to the emergence of the Dollar Wall-Street Regime: see especially 'East Asia's Dollars', *New Left Review*, II/40 (2006) and 'Bubblenomics', ibid., II/57 (2009).

87 For example, M. Dooley et al., 'The Revived Bretton Woods System', *International Journal of Finance and Economics*, 9 (2004).

88 Wolf, *Fixing Global Finance*, p. 124.

89 L. Panitch and M. Konings, 'Finance and American Empire', in *idem*, eds, *American Empire and the Political Economy of Global Finance*, p. 39.

90 Wolf, *Fixing Global Finance*, p. 126.
91 Ibid., pp. 137, 112, 100. Herman Schwarz argues the position of a hegemonic state is underpinned economically by it acting as the main market for other participants in the world economy: *States versus Markets* (2nd edn, Basingstoke, 2000) ch. 3.
92 L. Wittgenstein, *Philosophical Investigations* (Oxford, 1968), II.xi, p. 194.
93 For a brilliant contemporary analysis, see M. Davis, 'The Political Economy of Late Imperial America', *New Left Review*, I/143 (1984) and 'Reaganomics' Magical Mystery Tour', ibid., I/149 (1985).
94 See Greenspan's account of the two episodes in *The Age of Turbulence*, pp. 100–10, 187–96.
95 Panitch and Konings, 'Finance and American Empire', p. 40. For a more detailed, and nuanced development of the same idea, see C. Rude, 'The Role of Financial Discipline in Imperial Strategy', in Panitch and Konings, eds, *American Empire and the Political Economy of Global Finance*.
96 For example, R. H. Wade and F. Veneroso 'The Asian Crisis: The High-Debt Model versus the Wall Street-Treasury-IMF Complex', *New Left Review*, I/228 (1998).
97 Bryan and Rafferty, *Capitalism with Derivatives*, p. 132; see also ibid., ch. 7.
98 Mohun, 'Distributive Shares in the US Economy, 1964–2001', p. 360. See also G. Duménil and D. Lévy, 'Neoliberal Income Trends', *New Left Review*, II/30 (2004).
99 Giovanni Arrighi advances the idea of a late-twentieth-century–early-twenty-first-century *belle époque* in the context of an argument that the crisis of a hegemonic power (the US today, Britain a hundred years ago) tends to be accompanied by financialization and greater economic instability: *Adam Smith in Beijing* (London, 2007), ch. 6; but, even when detached from this cyclical theory, the idea is a suggestive one.
100 B. Bernanke, 'The Great Moderation', 20 February 2004, www.federalreserve.gov.
101 Panitch and Konings, 'Finance and American Empire', pp. 39–40. The 2008 financial crash led them to change their tune somewhat: see L. Panitch and M. Koonings, 'Myths of Deregulation', *New Left Review*, II/57 (2009).

102 See E. Luttwak, *Turbo-Capitalism* (London, 1998), ch. 11; and, for an example of the neoliberal critique of democracy, S. Brittan, 'The Economic Contradictions of Democracy', *British Journal of Political Science*, 5 (1975). As Luttwak points out, 'central bankism' to some degree represented a return to the 1920s, when Montagu Norman, Governor of the Bank of England, orchestrated an international network of powerful central and private bankers; for a popular account, see Ahamad, *Lords of Finance*. The failure of monetarism is diagnosed by Brittan in *How to Settle the 'Monetarist' Controversy* (London, 1982). See the critique of the neoliberal economic policy regime by a former practitioner, Sir John Gieve, ex-Deputy Governor of the Bank of England, 'Central Banks Need to Stop Fighting the Last War', *Financial Times*, 11 May 2009.

103 Brenner, *The Boom and the Bubble*, pp. 175–6; see also ibid., chs. 7 and 8.

104 R. Brenner, 'Towards the Precipice', *London Review of Books*, 6 February 2003.

105 Greenspan, *The Age of Turbulence*, p. 229.

106 R. Brenner, 'New Boom, New Bubble', *New Left Review*, II/25 (2004), p. 70.

107 J. Pickard et al., 'How US Housing Boom may be Coming to a Tricky End', *Financial Times*, 23 October 2006.

108 Tett, *Fool's Gold*, p. 146.

109 International Monetary Fund, *World Economic Outlook*, October 2007, www.imf.org, p. 67.

110 Ibid., p. 69.

111 G. Turner, *The Credit Crunch* (London, 2008), ch. 6.

112 D. Pilling, 'China's Export Dependency Has to Change', *Financial Times*, 26 May 2009.

113 B. Bernanke, 'The Global Savings Glut and the US Current Account Deficit', 10 March 2005, www.federalreserve.gov. See the critique in Turner, *The Credit Crunch*, ch. 4.

114 P. Augar, *Chasing Alpha: How Reckless Growth and Unchecked Ambition Ruined the City's Golden Decade* (London, 2009), p. 34.

115 *The Turner Review*, p. 21.

116 E. Luce, 'US Banks Spent $370m to Fight Rules' and 'Few Escape Blame Over Subprime Explosion', *Financial Times*, 6 May 2009.

117 F. Tregenna, 'The Fat Years: The Structure and Profitability of the US Banking Sector in the Pre-Crisis Period', *Cambridge Journal of Economics*, 33 (2009). For two fascinating, though very different bottom up accounts of US investment banking in this era, see K. Ho, *Liquidated: An Ethnography of Wall Street* (Durham NC, 2009) and L. McDonald, *A Colossal Failure of Common Sense: The Incredible Inside Story of the Collapse of Lehman Brothers* (New York, 2009).

118 Augar, *Chasing Alpha*, pp. 60–1, 118.

119 Tett, *Fool's Gold*, pp. 107–8. This is an example of what Trotsky called the privilege of backwardness.

120 Augar, *Chasing Alpha*, pp. 47, 142.

121 For example, W. Godley and A. Izurieta, 'As the Implosion Begins . . . ?', July 2001, and, most recently, W. Godley et al., 'The US Economy: Is There a Way Out of the Woods?', November 2007, www.levy.org.

122 C. Harman, *Capitalism's New Crisis* (London, 2008); Turner, *The Credit Crunch*, pp. 26–7.

123 Wolf, *Fixing Global Finance*, p. 69.

124 Ibid., p. 104.

125 Ibid., p. 104.

126 E. Luce, 'Stuck in the Middle', *Financial Times*, 28 October 2008.

127 Graham Turner in his admirable *The Credit Crunch* argues that housing bubbles were a means of maintaining demand and thereby of counteracting the effects of 'wage compression' caused by globalization. While this argument is fundamentally correct, it suffers from not being located in a deep enough analysis of the long-term crisis of overaccumulation and profitability and therefore tends to present the problem as one of the policy mistakes committed by the Fed and other central banks. See, for a somewhat similar criticism from a different perspective, Murphy, 'Bubblenomics'.

128 Wolf, *Fixing Global Finance*, p. 64.

129 Robin Blackburn provides a good critical account of the first phase of the crisis: 'The Subprime Crisis', *New Left Review*, II/50 (2008).

130 G. Tett, 'Should Atlas Still Shrug? The Threat That Lurks Behind the Growth of Complex Debt Deals', *Financial*

Times, 15 January 2007 – in the light of subsequent developments a remarkably prescient article.

131 M. Nakamoto and D. Wighton, 'Bullish Citigroup is "Still Dancing" to the Beat of the Buyout Boom', *Financial Times*, 10 July 2007.

132 Tett, *Fool's Gold*, pp. 172–3.

133 These illusions are recorded in S. Tucker et al., 'Asia's Continued Rise Spurs "Decoupling" Debate', *Financial Times*, 1 November 2007.

134 OECD *Economic Outlook: Interim Report*, March 2009, www.oecd.org, pp. 57, 19, 9.

135 J. Anderlini, 'Chinese Spending is Lifting Economy', *Financial Times*, 16 April 2009.

136 Minsky, *Stabilizing an Unstable Economy*, p. 132.

137 OECD *Economic Outlook: Interim Report*, March 2009, ch. 3.

138 IMF, *World Economic Outlook*, April 2009, ch. 3 (quotations from p. 98).

139 For detailed comparisons, see Box 3.1 'How Similar is the Current Crisis to the Great Depression?', ibid., pp. 99–103, C. Harman, 'The Slump of the 1930s and the Crisis Today', *International Socialism*, 2.121 (2009), and B. Eichengreen and K. H. O'Rourke, 'A Tale of Two Depressions', 4 June 2009, www.voxeu.org.

140 R. Koo, *The Holy Grail of Macroeconomics: Lessons from Japan's Great Recession* (Singapore, 2008), quotations from pp. 28, 29. This analysis leads Koo to reject what has become the orthodox interpretation of the Great Depression, influenced by Milton Friedman's and Anna Schwartz's famous study in *A Monetary History of the United States, 1867–1960* (Princeton, 1963), which explains the severity and depth of the crisis by the fall in the US money supply by over a third in 1929–33 as a consequence of the restrictive policy pursued by the Fed: see ch. 7, 'The Great Contraction'. Koo argues that the drop in the money supply was a consequence of declining demand for loans as firms sought to reduce their debts: *The Holy Grail of Macroeconomics*, ch. 3. For a partially parallel analysis that also involves a critique of the monetarist interpretation, see Dow, *Major Recessions*, pp. 157–83, 211–16.

141 Koo, *The Holy Grail of Macroeconomics*, p. 33.

142 International Monetary Fund, *Global Financial Stability Report*, April 2009, www.imf.org, p. 7.

143 Ibid., pp. 27, 34, 44. These staggering figures may still be an underestimate. The stress tests of the nineteen bank groups responsible for 70 per cent of American banking assets by the US regulators, whose results were announced in May 2009, estimated that their net losses in 2009–10 would be $535bn, more than the IMF's projection ($321bn) but lower than that by Nouriel Roubini, the notoriously accurate prophet of economic doom ($811bn): D.J. Elliott, 'Implications of the Bank Stress Tests', 11 May 2009, www.brookings.edu. But considerable uncertainty surrounds these figures: the IMF reduced its estimate of overall losses to $3.4 trillion in its October 2009 *Global Financial Stability Report*.

144 W. Munchau, 'Europe Must Learn from Japan's Experience', *Financial Times*, 4 May 2009.

145 See the fascinating account of these debates in E. A. Rosen, *Roosevelt, the Great Depression, and the Economics of Recovery* (Charlottesville, 2005). For a massive recent study of US international strategy after 1918, see P. O. Cohrs, *The Unfinished Peace after World War I: America, Britain and the Stabilization of Europe 1919–1932* (Cambridge, 2006), and, on Roosevelt's early Wilsonianism, R. Dallek, *Franklin Roosevelt and American Foreign Policy, 1932–1945* (rev. edn; New York, 1995), 'Prologue: An American Internationalist'.

146 J. Strachey, *A Programme for Progress* (London, 1940), pp. 226, 223, 225; see generally, ibid., ch. XVI, which includes an interesting discussion of debates within the administration. This book represented Strachey's conversion to Keynesian economics. Figures from C. P. Kindleberger, *The World in Depression 1929–1939* (rev. edn, 1987), p. 272. See ibid., ch. 12, on the 1937–8 recession; and, for a contrasting view, Rosen, *Roosevelt, the Great Depression, and the Economics of Recovery*, pp. 180–3.

147 Koo, *The Holy Grail of Macroeconomics*, pp. 117, 51–5.

148 Figures from OECD *Economic Outlook: Interim Report*, March 2009, Table 3.1, p. 110.

149 Lex, 'Latvia's Currency Peg', *Financial Times*, 1 June 2009.

150 J. Reed, 'Back on the Road', *Financial Times*, 18 June 2009.
151 N. N. Taleb, 'Ten Principles for a Black Swan-Proof World', *Financial Times*, 7 April 2009.
152 C. Freeland, 'Soros Calls Wall Street Profits "Gifts" from the State', *Financial Times*, 23 October 2009. See also G. Bowley, 'Bailout Helps Fuel a New Era of Wall Street Wealth', *New York Times*, 17 October 2009.
153 K. Rogoff, 'Why We Need to Regulate the Banks Sooner, Not Later', *Financial Times*, 19 August 2009.
154 N. Ferguson, *Too Big to Live: Why We Must Stamp Out State Monopoly Capitalism*, October 2009, www.cps.org,uk, p. 15. For a thought-provoking Marxist analysis, see G. Balakrishnan, 'Speculations on the Stationary State', *New Left Review*, II/59 (2009).
155 See Buiter's blog, www.blogs.ft.com/maverecon/.
156 K. Guha, 'Poser for Paulson: the US Treasury Chief Wants a Halt to Public Bailouts', *Financial Times*, 12 September 2008.
157 D. M. Herszenhorn et al., 'Talks Implode During a Day of Chaos', *New York Times*, 26 September 2008.
158 N. Roubini, 'Mother of All Carry Trades Faces an Inevitable Bust', *Financial Times*, 1 November 2009.

2 Empire Confined

1 J. Rosenberg, *The Follies of Globalization Theory* (London, 2000); see also D. Held, A. McGrew et al., *Global Transformations* (Cambridge, 1999); M. Hardt and A. Negri, *Empire* (Cambridge MA, 2000); and, for an overview of the globalization debate, A. Callinicos, *Social Theory* (2nd edn; Cambridge, 2007), ch. 13.
2 G. Friedman, '2008 and the Return of the State', 27 October 2008, www.stratfor.com.
3 *Financial Times*, 24 January 2003.
4 'The Divided West: Part Two', *Financial Times*, 28 May 2003.
5 E. Crooks, 'Uneasy Reliance on Russia Likely to Persist', *Financial Times*, 5 September 2008.
6 W. Munchau, 'German Complacency Poses a Serious Threat', *Financial Times*, 30 November 2008.

7 J. Wilson et al., 'Bundesbank Chief Hits Out at Brussels', *Financial Times*, 22 April 2009.
8 W. Munchau, 'Narrow-Minded Leadership Hurts Europe', *Financial Times*, 15 February 2009.
9 T. Barber, 'Precarious Podium', *Financial Times*, 18 March 2009.
10 Friedman, '2008 and the Return of the State'.
11 K. Guha and D. Pimlott, 'Banks Cut Back on Overseas Lending', *Financial Times*, 29 April 2009.
12 E. Gamberoni and R. Newfather, 'Trade Protection: Incipient but Worrying Trends', *Trade Notes*, 2 March 2009, www.worldbank.org; S. O'Connor, 'US Companies Hit by Repercussions of Buy American', *Financial Times*, 26 May 2009.
13 C. Dow, *Major Recessions: Britain and the World, 1920–1995* (Oxford, 1998), p. 179. See also C. P. Kindleberger, *The World in Depression 1929–1939* (rev. edn; Harmondsworth, 1987), pp. 123–7.
14 P. Marsh, 'Make and Mend: Reindustrializing Britain', *Financial Times*, 8 February 2009.
15 J. Lanchester, 'It's Finished', *London Review of Books*, 28 May 2009, p. 10.
16 R. Atkins, 'Germany's Policy of Containment', *Financial Times*, 6 April 2009.
17 Munchau, 'German Complacency Poses a Serious Threat'. More generally see G. Friedman, 'The United States, Germany and Beyond', 30 March 2009, www.stratfor. com.
18 See Marx's pioneering analysis in his account of the struggle to regulate the working day during the Industrial Revolution, *Capital*, I (Harmondsworth, 1976), ch. 10, and J. Holloway and S. Picciotto, eds., *The State and Capital* (London, 1977).
19 Friedman, '2008 and the Return of the State'.
20 *The Turner Review: A Regulatory Response to the Global Banking Crisis*, March 2009, www.fsa.gov.uk, p. 100.
21 L. D. Trotsky, *The First Five Years of the Communist International* (2 vols., New York, 1972), I, p. 23.
22 See D. Harvey, *The New Imperialism* (Oxford, 2003), and A. Callinicos, *Imperialism and Global Political Economy* (Cambridge, 2009).

23 See Harvey, *The New Imperialism*, A. Callinicos, *The New Mandarins of American Power* (Cambridge, 2003) and *Imperialism and Global Political Economy*, ch. 5, and, for an astringent conservative take that emphasizes the continuities between the global policy of the younger Bush's administration and those of its two immediate predecessors, A. J. Bacevich, *American Empire* (Cambridge MA, 2002).

24 R. Kagan, 'America's Crisis of Legitimacy', *Foreign Affairs*, March/April 2004.

25 T. E. Ricks, *The Gamble: General Petraeus and the Untold Story of the American Surge in Iraq, 2006–2008* (London, 2009), p. 9.

26 National Intelligence Council, *Global Trends 2025: A World Transformed*, November 2008, www.dni.gov, p. vi.

27 Ibid., p. 8.

28 Figures in this paragraph from Callinicos, *Imperialism and Global Political Economy*, Tables 4.1, 5.1, 5.4, pp. 147, 195, 208.

29 P. M. Kennedy, *The Rise and Fall of the Great Powers* (London, 1988).

30 F. Fukuyama, 'The Fall of America, Inc.', *Newsweek*, 13 October 2008. Fukuyama abjured neoconservatism in *After the Neocons: America at the Crossroads* (London, 2006). For an astringent critique of this recantation and its limits, see P. Anderson, 'Inside Man', *The Nation*, 6 April 2006.

31 R. Dallek, *Franklin Roosevelt and American Foreign Policy, 1932–1945* (rev. edn; New York, 1995), Parts 1 and 2.

32 K. Rogoff, 'America Will Need a $1,000bn Bail-Out', *Financial Times*, 18 September 2008.

33 G. Dyer, 'China's Dollar Dilemma', *Financial Times*, 23 February 2009.

34 G. Dyer, 'Wen "Worried" about China's US Assets', *Financial Times*, 13 March 2009.

35 NIC, *Global Trends 2025*, vi. See the comparison with its earlier report, ibid., p. 2.

36 D. Harvey, 'Why the US Stimulus Package is Bound to Fail', *The Bullet*, 12 February 2009, www.socialistproject.ca. See G. Arrighi, *The Long Twentieth Century* (London, 1994) and *Adam Smith in Beijing* (London, 2007).

37 See, in addition to the texts cited in notes 22 and 23 above, A. Callinicos, 'Marxism and Imperialism Today', *International Socialism*, 2.50 (1991), and 'Imperialism and Global Political Economy', ibid., 2.108 (2005). Simon Bromley's fine book *American Power and the Prospects for International Order* (Cambridge, 2008), though couched as a challenge to more radical analyses such as Harvey's and mine, does not seem to differ much in substantive judgements from the analysis developed here.

38 For a brief discussion of this debate, see Callinicos, *Imperialism and Global Political Economy*, pp. 198–9.

39 N. Ferguson, 'An Imaginary Retrospective of 2009', *Financial Times*, 27 December 2008.

40 M. Wolf, 'Japanese Lessons for a World of Balance-Sheet Deflation', *Financial Times*, 18 February 2009.

41 F. Zakaria, *The Post-American World* (London, 2008), p. 165.

42 J. Authers, 'Another Brick in China's Great Wall of Confusion', *Financial Times*, 31 July 2009. On Chinese statistics, see also A. Wolfe and R. Ziemba, 'China's GDP Growth and Electricity Contraction: Not a Contradiction After All?', 15 July 2009, *Asia EconoMonitor*, www.rgemonitor. com, and J. Anderlini, 'China's Growth Figures Fail to Add Up', *Financial Times*, 4 August 2009.

43 Lex, 'China Stimulus', *Financial Times*, 25 November 2008.

44 R. McGregor, 'Beijing Risks Passing on a Poisoned Chalice', *Financial Times*, 10 August 2009.

45 See Ho-fung Hung, 'Rise of China and the Global Overaccumulation Crisis', *Review of International Political Economy*, 15 (2008). Writing from a neoclassical perspective, Yasheng Huang paints a fascinating portrait of the complexity and contradictions of the Chinese economy, in which he shows the state continues to play a central role: *Capitalism with Chinese Characteristics* (Cambridge, 2008).

46 D. McNally, 'From Financial Crisis to World Slump', *Historical Materialism*, 17.2 (2009), p. 64.

47 D. Oakley, 'Decoupling Gains Brand New Group of Cheerleaders', *Financial Times*, 12 June 2009.

48 G. Dyer, 'China Rebound Hinges on Role of Exports', *Financial Times*, 15 April 2009.

49 D. Pilling, 'Asia and the Crisis: Unlucky Numbers', *Financial Times*, 13 February 2009.

50 The importance of the latter feature is highlighted in R. Walker and D. Buck, 'The Chinese Road', *New Left Review*, II/46 (2007).

51 Zakaria, *The Post-American World*, pp. 232–3; reference to W. C. Wolforth, 'The Stability of a Unipolar World', *International Security*, 21 (1999). See also Callinicos, *Imperialism and Global Political Economy*, pp. 213–17.

52 S. Žižek, 'Use Your Illusions', *London Review of Books*, 14 November 2008.

53 Z. Brzezinski, *The Choice: Global Domination or Global Leadership* (New York, 2004).

54 'Remarks of President Barack Obama, Address to Joint Session of Congress', 24 February 2009, www.whitehouse.gov.

55 G. Friedman, 'Munich and the Continuity between the Bush and Obama Foreign Policies', 9 February 2009, www.stratfor.com.

56 P. Anderson, 'Jottings on the Conjuncture', *New Left Review*, II/48 (2007), p. 11.

57 See, for example, J. Lamont and A. Kazmin, 'Fear of Influence', *Financial Times*, 13 July 2009.

58 S. Romero and A. Barrionuevo, 'Deal by Deal, China Expands Its Influence in Latin America', *New York Times*, 15 April 2009.

Conclusion: Regime Change or System Change?

1 R. H. Wade, 'Financial Regime Change?', *New Left Review*, II/53 (2008), pp. 6–7.

2 Ibid., pp. 20–1. See also the slightly later and more extensive version of the same diagnosis in *idem*, 'From Global Imbalances to Global Reorganization', *Cambridge Journal of Economics*, 33 (2009).

3 'Nationalize to Save the Free Market', *Financial Times*, 13 October 2008.

4 M. Wolf, 'Seeds of Its Own Destruction', *Financial Times*, 8 March 2009.

5 M. Wolf, 'This Crisis is a Moment, but is It a Defining One?', *Financial Times*, 19 May 2009.

6 J. G. Ruggie, 'International Regimes, Transactions, and Change: Embedded Liberalism in the Postwar Economic Order', *International Organizations*, 32 (1982), p. 393. See also K. Polanyi *The Great Transformation* (Boston, 1957).

7 M. Wolf, 'Is America the New Russia?', *Financial Times*, 14 April 2009.

8 Wade, 'Financial Regime Change?', p. 21.

9 A. Callinicos, 'Does Capitalism Need the State System?', *Cambridge Review of International Affairs*, 20 (2007), and *Imperialism and Global Political Economy* (Cambridge, 2009), ch. 2.

10 See F. Block, 'The Ruling Class Does Not Rule', in *idem*, *Revising State Theory* (Philadelphia, 1987); C. Harman, 'The State and Capitalism Today', *International Socialism*, 2.51 (1991); R. Miliband, 'State Power and Class Interests', *New Left Review*, I/138 (1983); and C. Offe, and V. Ronge, 'Theses on the Theory of the State', in A. Giddens and D. Held, eds, *Classes, Power, and Conflict* (Berkeley/Los Angeles, 1982).

11 H. Minsky, *Stabilizing an Unstable Economy* (New York, 2008), p. 106.

12 For a critical assessment of Chávez's record, see M. Gonzalez, 'Chávez Ten Years On', *International Socialism*, 2.121 (2009).

13 J. Holloway, *Change the World without Taking Power* (London, 2002). This section draws on A. Callinicos, 'Alternatives to Neoliberalism', *Socialist Review*, July 2006.

14 See J. Holloway and A. Callinicos, 'Can We Change the World without Taking Power?', *International Socialism*, 1.106 (2005).

15 See G. Gordon, 'President Evo Morales' Gas and Oil "Nationalization" Decree', June 2006, www.democracyctr. org.

16 H. Draper, *Karl Marx's Theory of Revolution*, I (New York, 1977), and A. Callinicos, *The Revolutionary Ideas of Karl Marx* (London, 1983).

17 A. Artous, '*Democracy against Capitalism*: On the book by Thomas Coutrot', *International Socialist Tendency Discussion Bulletin*, no. 7, January 2006, www.istendency.net, p. 10.

18 D. Miller, *Market, State, and Community* (Oxford, 1989); J. Roemer, *A Future for Socialism* (London, 1994); and T. Smith, *Globalization: A Systematic Marxian Account* (Brill, 2006), ch. 8.

19 M. Albert, *Parecon: Life after Capitalism* (London, 2003), p. 70.

20 For much more on this crucial subject, see G. Monbiot, *Heat* (London, 2006), J. Neale, *Stop Global Warming: Change the World* (London, 2008) and J. B. Foster, *The Ecological Revolution* (New York, 2009).

21 P. Devine, *Democracy and Economic Planning* (Cambridge, 1988). I discuss this book in *An Anti-Capitalist Manifesto* (Cambridge, 2003), ch. 3, and Parecon in my debate with Albert, 'Movement Building 2004: Vision and Strategy', available at www.zmag.org and www.swp.org. uk.

22 K. Marx, 'Critique of the Gotha Programme', in Marx and Engels, *Collected Works*, XXIV (London, 1989), p. 87.

23 See the discussion of basic income in A. Callinicos, *Equality* (London, 2000), pp. 114–18, and, for a somewhat broader programme than that discussed here, Callinicos, *An Anti-Capitalist Manifesto*, pp. 132–40.

24 See, for example, R. Zibechi, 'El Alto: The Heights of the Bolivian Movement', *Socialist Worker*, 22 April 2006.

Index